The Authenticity of the Second Letter to the Thessalonians

The Authenticity of the Second Letter to the Thessalonians

William Wrede

Translated by
Robert Rhea

James Clarke & Co

James Clarke & Co
P.O. Box 60
Cambridge
CB1 2NT
United Kingdom

www.jamesclarke.co
publishing@jamesclarke.co

ISBN: 978 0 227 17691 7

British Library Cataloguing in Publication Data
A record is available from the British Library

First published by James Clarke & Co, 2018
Copyright © Robert B. Rhea, 2017

Published by arrangement
with Cascade Books

All rights reserved. No part of this edition may be reproduced, stored electronically or in any retrieval system, or transmitted in any form or by any means, electronic, mechanical, photocopying, recording, or otherwise, without prior written permission from the Publisher (permissions@jamesclarke.co).

To my mother Sara who understood the beauteous natural world with all its plants, flowers, shrubs, trees, the skies above and all creatures above and below the waters to be a wondrous reflection of heaven, a truly vibrant, marvelous manifestation of the Divine Love permeated by earthly light, glory, and splendor which mirror throughout the earth the radiance of our Lord and Lady, Jesus of Galilee and the Queen of Heaven.

To my sister Ann and her family for their tolerance of the many ways of my life's journey.

CONTENTS

Translator's Preface | ix
Translator's Note | xi
Acknowledgments | xiii
Abbreviations for Reference Works | xiv
Notes on the Greek | xv
Preface | xvii

Preliminary Remarks | 1

Chapter I

The Literary Relationship of the Two Letters to the Thessalonians: A Comparison of the Parallels | 4

> An overview of the parallels. General comments. The unique parallel structure of the two letters. The historical setting and situation. The content of the two letters. The structure and formation. The parallels occur in parallel sections of the letters. Some parallels appear in conspicuously corresponding verses and passages. The sequence of the parallels is predominately the same. Exact parallelism can be documented between 1 Thess 1:1 and 2 Thess 1:1–2; 1 Thess 2:9 and 2 Thess 3:8. The results of this comparison can only be explained on the basis of the literary use of the first letter by the writer of the second letter. Paul is not the author. The difference between the two letters. Timothy is not the author.

Chapter II

Objections to an Early Fiction: The Writer's Purpose and Situation | 35

> The second letter rejects the expectation of the imminent Coming of the Parousia. The oppositional relationship between 1 Thess 5:1–4 and 2 Thess 2:1–12. The preaching of the End Time has caused great fright and concern. The influence of the prophets has yielded nothing for the present situation. The mention of persecutions has also

not had an effect. Can Paul himself refer only to a forged letter with 2 Thess 2:2? But 2 Thess 2:2 is not comprehensible as a Pauline assertion. If 2 Thess 2:2 is not of Pauline origin, then it does not refer to a forged letter. Διὰ λόγου and 2 Thess 2:2. The result of the exegesis. (The reason for a letter to the Thessalonians) The overall historical relationship. The authority of the Pauline letters creates difficulties. (2 Pet 3:16; Jas 2:14ff).

Chapter III
Literary Form and Composition | 70

Remarks concerning parlance and modes of expression. The mood and tone of the letter. The characteristic literary techniques of the forger. The use of "I" and "we" in the letters. The plausibility of the assumed forgery. Ambiguity as a consequence of the forgery.

Chapter IV
The Letter as Forgery | 83

The applicability and practicality of the concept of a forgery. 2 Thess 3:17 does not contradict because it is deliberately deceptive. The success of the forgery. A Possible Chronology. There is no definite *terminus a quo.* The attestation of the letter by Marcion and Polycarp. A later evaluation and use of 2 Thess 2:4 appears questionable and dubious.

Chapter V
The Significance of the Jerusalem Temple | 93

The Temple and not the Church. The content of 2 Thess 2:3–12 is not the fabrication of the author. There is perhaps a literary source for this passage. The expectation of 2 Thess 2:4 also can have been derived from an older concept. The reinterpretation of the words about the temple cannot be assumed. It is difficult to presuppose the reconstruction of the Temple. Has this usage been taken over and adopted without the thought of the destruction of the Temple? What are the possible, related analogies? (Rev 11:1, 2, 8, 13.) The result.

Bibliography | 112

TRANSLATOR'S PREFACE

Wrede tells us in the preface to his study of the Second Letter to the Thessalonians that for a certain time he could not decide for or against the authenticity of this letter that tradition ascribes to the Apostle Paul. Unlike those scholars who had used the eschatological argument to reach a "definite" decision for or against authenticity, he was never satisfied with it and did not consider that argument to be definitive. One must assume that though he had doubts, he must have always held the suspicion that the letter was not Paul's but could not quite put his finger on those characteristics of it that gave rise to this opinion. It seems that he must have spent a rather long time with the attempt to find a more precise way to describe and document a definite factual approach to the dilemma.

It must have been that as he began juxtaposing the verses of the two letters to the Thessalonians, placing them side by side in the order that they occurred in their respective texts, he happened upon what for him became the most vaild solution. Not only was he able to locate some exact parallels of words, phrases, and sentences, he also could find definite related words, verses, and related passages that precisely mirrored and reflected their counterparts in the First Letter to the Thessalonians. What must have been the final discovery was the related structure of the two letters that enabled him to declare at long last, "Eureka." Wrede's order of the Greek parallels has been reproduced with his original annotations in this translation; for since they form the foundation of his argument, it was deemed essential to present them in the manner in which he laid them out.

This sense of discovery permeates his study, particularly the first chapter, but it extends also throughout this work. Even when he addresses the possible origin of this letter and its destination, he continues the adventure by postulating that it may have been written in Phrygia where within in a short amount of time it was added to the collection of Paul's letters in

Translator's Preface

surrounding Christian communities before it eventually found its way to Rome where Marcion added it to his *Apostolikon*. As I translated the text, it was this perceived sense of excitement of his that made the endeavor a captivating one. It seemed each day he took me on another adventure as though he were telling a story, even though he was writing an exegetical study.

Robert B. Rhea
Bristol, Tennessee
June 2016

TRANSLATOR'S NOTE

Wrede did not prepare and append a bibliography to his study of the Second Letter to the Thessalonians. Rather he placed fragmentary footnotes at the bottom of a page, and thus much of what today is expected for a complete footnote was not included. From the bibliographical data that he reported, it is evident that he sought only to guide the reader to an author and a source; and often he did not give the name of a publisher, the date of publication, or title or range of pages for periodical entries.

The bibliography for this translation has been compiled from entries taken from Wrede's original footnotes. For those periodical entries for which he did not give the title of the article and sometimes when he did not give even the title of a monograph, I have used the designation, "untitled entry," followed by the title of the journal or other publication cited.

From time to time he used abbreviations but did not attach a list of abbreviations with their corresponding full titles. For these entries I have had no other alternative but to simply list the abbreviations. Nonetheless my incomplete bibliography and list of abbreviations give the reader a better overview of this material than Wrede's original footnotes to his text.

ACKNOWLEDGMENTS

The Rev. Harry Shaefer suggested this project, typed Wrede's Greek into the SBL polytonic font, and proofread the entire manuscript. Susan Kotlinski proofread the Greek. Paolo Livieri compared the translation with the original German.

We would like to especially thank the Rev. Dr. Richard Ray, interim president, and the IT Department of King University, Bristol, Tennessee for their kind cooperation with the use of their facilities for the completion of much of this project.

ABBREVIATIONS FOR REFERENCE WORKS

HNT	*Handkommentar zum Neuen Testament.*
JPT	*Jahrbuch für protestanische Theologie.* 1880.
LNTT	*Lehrbuch der Neutestamentliche Theologie.*
MK	*Das Meyersche Kommentar.* 5th and 6th ed.
NTS	*Neutestamentliche Studien.*
NZHT	*Niedners Zeitschrift für historische Theologie.* 1851.
PA	*Patr Apost.*
PAO	*Patr Apost Opp.*
SBL	*Schenkels Bibellexikon.*
SK	*Studien und Kritiken.* 1850.
TJ	*Theologisches Jahrbuch.* 1848.
TLZ	*Theologische Literatur Zeitung.* 1891.
TSSO	*Theologische Studien und Skizzen aus Ostpreussen.* 1889.
TUU	*Texte und Untersuchungen.*
TZT	*Tübinger Zeitschrift für Theologie.* 1839.
ZKWKL	*Zeitschrift für kirchliche Wissenschaft und kirchliches Leben.* 1886.
ZNTW	*Zeitschrift für die Neutestamentliche Wissenschaft.*
ZWT	*Zeitschrift für die wissenschaftliche Theologie.* 1862.

NOTES ON THE GREEK

It has been our intention to reproduce Wrede's use of the Nestle Aland Greek text of the New Testament, except for some obvious typographical errors:

* In 2 Thess 1:7 Wrede has incorrectly place a period between τοῖς and θλίβουσιν.
* In 1 Thess 1:3, Wrede has incorrectly written παιτρὸς.
* For 1 Thess 4:5–6, the heading is correct, but Wrede has mislabelled verse 5 as 6 and verse 6 as 7.
* Footnote 46 on page 55 referencing Spitta, *Zur Geschichte* quotes 2 Thess 3:11 incorrectly, putting a semi-colon after τινας.
* On page 9, Wrede incorrectly has κατευθύναι ἡμῶν τὰς καρδιάς, which we have corrected to read ὑμῶν.

Otherwise, we have followed the Greek text that is in the German edition of *Die Echtheit*.

PREFACE

The following exegetical study was already completed as I began the writing of my book on *The Messianic Secret in the Gospels* (Göttingen, 1901) more than two years ago except for some comments that I have since completed. Meanwhile H. Holtzmann's article, "On the Second Letter to the Thessalonians," appeared in the *Zeitschrift für die Neutestamentliche Wissenachaft,* II 1901, S. 97–108. Since likewise in his work as in mine the relationship of the Second Letter to the Thessalonians to the First Letter to the Thessalonians is particularly discussed, the question could arise as to whether or not my study is pertinent to the debate. On that matter I have not fostered any doubt. My study is so completely different from Holtzmann's work with regard to content, composition, and conception that I would have written it in any event, even if I had been familiar with his article. With regard to the revision and editing of my entire study, which I completed for its publication, I found that only a few significant additions and a series of formal revisions were necessary.

Perhaps the presentation in Chapter I is too expansive for some readers. However, here where the foundation of the argument is dealt with, I have wanted to present the facts as precisely as possible.

With regard to the presentation of the problem of Chapter V—whoever knows better what might be said here, I would be very thankful for that person's viewpoint. Most valuable to me concerning this matter was H. Gunkel's comment, which he sent me via a letter, even though I could not accept his view.

The question concerning the authenticity of the Second Letter to the Thessalonians has only marginal significance for the history of early Christianity. Nonetheless this topic has a special meaning and fascination.

Preface

Almost against my will it has continued to intrigue me once I had approached it closely.

Breslau, December 1902
W. Wrede

PRELIMINARY REMARKS

With regard to the concern of biblical criticism that questions the authenticity of the Second Letter to the Thessalonians, E. Reuss[1] has missed the "striking primary argument." As H. Holtzmann sought to find it (the primary argument) in his description and study of the eschatological theme of the second chapter,[2] so he certainly gave expression to the prevailing opinion of the school of modern biblical criticism, as far as biblical criticism has generally disputed and questioned the Pauline origin of this little letter. Yet the efforts of the defense on the other hand have focused themselves thoroughly and predominantly on the same argument and topic.

It is my view that although certainly a suspicion can arise from the nature of the content and meaning of this passage, a thoroughly convincing argument against the Pauline origin and provenance of this letter does not allow itself to be documented on the basis of it. That which, for example, B. Bornemann,[3] Jülicher,[4] Zahn,[5] and, among other viewpoints, Gunkel[6] and Bousset[7] have written along these lines about the passage that presents the Anti-Christ is not so easily discounted. That the reference of the passage points to Nero has by all means been totally discarded. One realizes that the traits of the Anti-Christ are not to be found with this description, which would then reveal the Roman ruler, a mother-murderer, the *Redivivus*, and

---

1. Reuss, *Die Geschichte*, 73.
2. Holtzmann, *Lehrbuch*, 215.
3. Bornemann, *Die Thessalonicherbriefe*, 357ff.
4. Jülicher, *Einleitung*, 41ff., 48ff.
5. Zahn, *Einleitung*, 178ff.
6. Gunkel, *Schöpfung und Chaos*, 221ff.
7. Bousset, *Der Antichrist*, 13.

a persecutor of Christians. Then too the argument and claim that this chapter has been influenced by the Book of Revelation no longer so easily finds the reception and belief it once had.

Totally independent from the concept of the eschatological passage, one can find with substantially better results that very "striking primary argument" with another aspect and point: *in the literary relationship of the Second Letter to the First Letter of the Thessalonians*. Many scholars have hardly at all taken note of this relationship;[8] others have seriously examined it and have placed emphasis upon it; but without exception its meaning and significance have not been highly and properly enough evaluated by any of them.[9]

At least to me it appears that the matter is to be understood as follows. My judgment of this letter has wavered and swung back and forth for a rather long time. Yet a more exact and careful study of its relationship to the First Letter to the Thessalonians has led me to the viewpoint that its authenticity does not allow itself to be verified and sustained. However in this regard it is my opinion that despite all of the well-intended observations which have arisen from the comparison of these two letters, the strength of this argument has yet to become fully evident and understood, be that merely because one has not thoroughly enough collected, highlighted, followed up, and consequently pursued the observations that have been made. If I am mistaken about this, then the reader alone must decide.

Naturally it will not be possible to limit our study to only one aspect of the comparison. Then too much of what is often dealt with here will only be briefly touched on in this study; other aspects of the matter will require a detailed analysis and observation. Above all our effort should not remain with merely a negative assessment: it must be asked how this letter is to be positively understood and comprehended as document penned by pseudonym. Thus far biblical criticism has brought about valuable contributions to this question, but it has not attended to the matter with the same interest as it has with the formulation and substantiation of the negative

---

8. Klöpper, "Der zweite Brief." Also B. Weiss in his *Einleitung* deals briefly with this relationship.

9. Weizsäcker, *Der Apostolische Zeitalter*, 258. He makes this point a primary argument. On page 460 of his study, *Die Thessalonicherbriefe*, Bornemann finds this argument the most important but still maintains that the second letter is authentic. Holtzmann places special emphasis on this in his article, "Zum zweiten Thessalonicherbrief," but concludes that the apocalyptic expectation of the second letter remains the decisive element.

assessment.[10] Therefore, the scholarship has not sufficiently recognized and valued certain difficulties that stand in the way with regard to the dispute over the authenticity of the Second Letter to the Thessalonians.

---

10. Bornemann, *Die Thessalonicherbriefe*, 478. He states, ". . . previously those who debate the authenticity of the second letter have neither made the attempt nor sought to elaborate on it to make clear the unique character and the distinct content of the second letter under the presupposition of its fictitiousness."

CHAPTER I

THE LITERARY RELATIONSHIP OF THE TWO LETTERS TO THE THESSALONIANS
A Comparison of the Parallels

First of all, let us simply place once more, in a concise overview, the corresponding parallels that are to be found in both letters.

For our purposes it is best to move and place the pertinent passages and pericopes of the first letter next to those of the corresponding sections of the text of the second letter, all that is related—not simply similar verbal sounds but also random words and other similarities—so that they might be highlighted by the printed text, and then begin the discussion with a few comments of explanation. This overview will make clear which parallels must be viewed and considered together—for it depends upon those relationships, as it will become apparent. On the other hand, the overview will to a certain extent make clear in which relationship the parallels are to be viewed with regard to the unique character and content of each letter. By the way, we will not simply list every word or phrase that scholars have compared previously. Parallels such as 1 Thess 2:16 ἵνα σωθῶσιν and 2 Thess 2:10 εἰς τὸ σωθῆναι αὐτούς[1] or 1 Thess 2:11 ἕνα ἕκαστον and 2 Thess 1:3 ἑνὸς

---

1. Holtzmann, "Zum zweiten Thessalonicherbrief," 101. Additionally he also compares the οὐκ ἐδέξαντο before these words with the ἐδέξασθε of 1 Thess 2:13, although these three verses come before ἵνα σωθῶσιν and have a completely different object than the οὐκ ἐδέξαντο.

ἑκάστου will be intentionally omitted. However, it is my opinion that the overview will contain everything that is actually of any relevance for our question.[2]

2 Thess	1 Thess
1.1–2	1.1
1 <u>Παῦλος καὶ Σιλουανὸς καὶ Τιμόθεος τῇ ἐκκλησίᾳ Θεσσαλονικέων ἐν θεῷ πατρὶ ἡμῶν καὶ κυρίῳ Ἰησοῦ Χριστῷ</u>· 2 χάρις ὑμῖν καὶ εἰρήνη ἀπὸ θεοῦ πατρὸς [ἡμῶν] καὶ κυρίου Ἰησοῦ Χριστοῦ.	1 Παῦλος καὶ Σιλουανὸς καὶ Τιμόθεος τῇ ἐκκλησίᾳ Θεσσαλονικέων ἐν θεῷ πατρὶ καὶ κυρίῳ Ἰησοῦ Χριστῷ· χάρις ὑμῖν καὶ εἰρήνη.
	a) to verse 3f, 10f:
1.3–12	1.2–10
3 <u>Εὐχαριστεῖν</u> ὀφείλομεν <u>τῷ θεῷ πάντοτε περὶ ὑμῶν</u>, ἀδελφοί, καθὼς ἄξιόν ἐστιν, ὅτι ὑπεραυξάνει <u>ἡ πίστις</u> ὑμῶν καὶ <u>πλεονάζει</u> (b) <u>ἡ ἀγάπη</u> (a, b) ἑνὸς ἑκάστου πάντων ὑμῶν εἰς ἀλλήλους (b), 4 <u>ὥστε αὐτοὺς ἡμᾶς ἐν ὑμῖν ἐγκαυχᾶσθαι ἐν ταῖς ἐκκλησίαις τοῦ θεοῦ</u> (d) ὑπὲρ <u>τῆς ὑπομονῆς</u> ὑμῶν καὶ <u>πίστεως</u> ἐν πᾶσιν τοῖς <u>διωγμοῖς</u> (d) ὑμῶν <u>καὶ ταῖς θλίψεσιν</u> αἷς ἀνέχεσθε, 5 ἔνδειγμα τῆς δικαίας κρίσεως τοῦ θεοῦ, <u>εἰς τὸ καταξιωθῆναι</u> ὑμᾶς <u>τῆς βασιλείας τοῦ θεοῦ</u> (e), ὑπὲρ ἧς καὶ πάσχετε, 6 εἴπερ δίκαιον παρὰ θεῷ ἀνταποδοῦναι τοῖς θλίβουσιν ὑμᾶς θλῖψιν 7 καὶ ὑμῖν τοῖς θλιβομένοις ἄνεσιν μεθ' ἡμῶν, <u>ἐν τῇ ἀποκαλύψει τοῦ κυρίου Ἰησοῦ</u> (b) <u>ἀπ' οὐρανοῦ</u> (c) <u>μετ' ἀγγέλων</u> δυνάμεως <u>αὐτοῦ</u> 8 ἐν πυρὶ φλογός, <u>διδόντος ἐκδίκησιν τοῖς μὴ εἰδόσιν θεὸν</u> (f) καὶ τοῖς μὴ ὑπακούουσιν τῷ εὐαγγελίῳ τοῦ κυρίου ἡμῶν Ἰησοῦ, 9 οἵτινες δίκην τίσουσιν ὄλεθρον αἰώνιον ἀπὸ προσώπου τοῦ κυρίου καὶ ἀπὸ τῆς δόξης τῆς ἰσχύος αὐτοῦ, 10 ὅταν <u>ἔλθῃ</u> ἐνδοξασθῆναι <u>ἐν τοῖς ἁγίοις αὐτοῦ</u> (b) καὶ θαυμασθῆναι <u>ἐν πᾶσιν τοῖς πιστεύσασιν</u>, ὅτι ἐπιστεύθη τὸ μαρτύριον ἡμῶν ἐφ' ὑμᾶς, ἐν τῇ ἡμέρᾳ ἐκείνῃ. 11 <u>Εἰς ὃ καὶ προσευχόμεθα πάντοτε περὶ ὑμῶν</u>, ἵνα ὑμᾶς <u>ἀξιώσῃ τῆς κλήσεως ὁ θεὸς</u> (e) ἡμῶν καὶ πληρώσῃ πᾶσαν εὐδοκίαν ἀγαθωσύνης καὶ <u>ἔργον πίστεως</u> ἐν	2 <u>Εὐχαριστοῦμεν τῷ θεῷ πάντοτε</u> περὶ πάντων ὑμῶν. μνείαν ποιούμενοι <u>ἐπὶ τῶν προσευχῶν ἡμῶν</u>, 3 ἀδιαλείπτως μνημονεύοντες ὑμῶν τοῦ <u>ἔργου</u> τῆς <u>πίστεως</u> καὶ τοῦ κόπου τῆς <u>ἀγάπης</u> καὶ <u>τῆς ὑπομονῆς</u> τῆς ἐλπίδος τοῦ κυρίου ἡμῶν Ἰησοῦ Χριστοῦ ἔμπροσθεν τοῦ θεοῦ καὶ πατρὸς ἡμῶν, . . . 6 καὶ ὑμεῖς μιμηταὶ ἡμῶν ἐγενήθητε καὶ τοῦ κυρίου, δεξάμενοι τὸν λόγον ἐν <u>θλίψει</u> πολλῇ μετὰ χαρᾶς πνεύματος ἁγίου, 7 <u>ὥστε</u> γενέσθαι ὑμᾶς τύπον πᾶσιν τοῖς πιστεύουσιν ἐν τῇ Μακεδονίᾳ καὶ τῇ Ἀχαΐᾳ. 8 ἀφ' ὑμῶν γὰρ ἐξήχηται ὁ λόγος τοῦ κυρίου οὐ μόνον ἐν τῇ Μακεδονίᾳ καὶ Ἀχαΐᾳ, ἀλλ' <u>ἐν παντὶ τόπῳ ἡ πίστις ὑμῶν ἡ πρὸς τὸν θεὸν ἐξελήλυθεν</u>, ὥστε μὴ χρείαν ἔχειν ἡμᾶς λαλεῖν τι . . . .
	b) to verse 3, 7, 10:
	3.12–13
	12 ὑμᾶς δὲ ὁ κύριος <u>πλεονάσαι</u> καὶ περισσεύσαι <u>τῇ ἀγάπῃ εἰς ἀλλήλους</u> καὶ εἰς πάντας, καθάπερ καὶ ἡμεῖς εἰς ὑμᾶς, 13 εἰς τὸ στηρίξαι ὑμῶν τὰς καρδίας ἀμέμπτους ἐν ἁγιωσύνῃ ἔμπροσθεν τοῦ θεοῦ καὶ πατρὸς ἡμῶν <u>ἐν τῇ παρουσίᾳ τοῦ κυρίου ἡμῶν Ἰησοῦ μετὰ</u> πάντων <u>τῶν ἁγίων αὐτοῦ</u>.
	c) to verse 7 (where the text also mentions the arrival of Jesus):

---

2. The Greek text has been taken from Nestle's version of the Greek New Testament. The letters that refer to the corresponding verses in 1 Thessalonians have been added only when they facilitate the comparative orientation.

δυνάμει, 12 ὅπως ἐνδοξασθῇ τὸ ὄνομα τοῦ κυρίου ἡμῶν Ἰησοῦ ἐν ὑμῖν, καὶ ὑμεῖς ἐν αὐτῷ, κατὰ τὴν χάριν τοῦ θεοῦ ἡμῶν καὶ κυρίου Ἰησοῦ Χριστοῦ.	4.16 καταβήσεται <u>ἀπ' οὐρανοῦ</u> d) to verse 4 ff: 2.14 ff. 19 14 ὑμεῖς γὰρ μιμηταὶ ἐγενήθητε, ἀδελφοί, <u>τῶν ἐκκλησιῶν τοῦ θεοῦ</u> τῶν οὐσῶν ἐν τῇ Ἰουδαίᾳ . . . The following phrases speak of *persecution* and of *divine wrath*. 19 τίς γὰρ ἡμῶν ἐλπὶς ἢ χαρὰ ἢ στέφανος <u>καυχήσεως</u> ἢ οὐχὶ καὶ ὑμεῖς . . . ; e) to verse 5 and 11: 2.12 . . . καὶ μαρτυρόμενοι <u>εἰς τὸ περιπατεῖν</u> ὑμᾶς <u>ἀξίως τοῦ θεοῦ</u> τοῦ <u>καλοῦντος</u> ὑμᾶς εἰς τὴν ἑαυτοῦ <u>βασιλείαν</u> καὶ δόξαν. f) to verse 8: 4.5–6 . . . 6 μὴ ἐν πάθει ἐπιθυμίας καθάπερ καὶ τὰ ἔθνη <u>τὰ μὴ εἰδότα τὸν θεόν</u>, 7 τὸ μὴ ὑπερβαίνειν καὶ πλεονεκτεῖν . . . διότι <u>ἔκδικος κύριος</u> περὶ πάντων τούτων.

The primary parallel to the selected section of the second letter is 1 Thess 1:2–10. But on the contrary, the verses 5–9 in the second letter offer hardly anything that can be compared to this text of the first letter. The parallels are to be found first of all in the words of thanksgiving and petition of verses 3 and 11—which naturally means very little—, in the close sequence of the words πίστις, ἀγάπη, ὑπομονή, θλῖψις, in the expression, ἔργον πίστεως (1 Thess: τῆς πίστεως), which does not reoccur in any other Pauline passage, and in the phrase (ἐν) πᾶσιν τοῖς πιστεύσασιν (1 Thess: πιστεύουσιν), which here appears in another context as 1 Thess 1:7. The only thing worthy of note besides these word parallels is that the thought and meaning of verse 4 is closely related to 1 Thess 1:7–8. According to this passage, Paul proclaims the fame and glory of the Thessalonians, whereby he says that because of their faith they are seen as the model for all believers in Macedonia and Achaia and explains straightforwardly according to 2 Thess 1:4 that he himself—be it alone or with his followers (ἡμᾶς?)—prides himself on the Thessalonians among all of the other congregations of God on account of their faith.

Under f) may it be noted that the expression οἱ μὴ εἰδότες θεόν (1 Thess: τὰ ἔθνη τὰ μὴ εἰδότα θεόν), used for the Gentiles, occurs only in these two verses in all of Paul's letters.³ Similar, however, to Gal 4:8: ἀλλὰ τότε μὲν οὐκ εἰδότες θεὸν ἐδουλεύσατε τοῖς φύσει μὴ οὖσιν θεοῖς. Cf., by the way, to LXX Jer 10:25 and also Ps 79:6 (78).

It should also be mentioned here under b) that ἀγάπη with πλεονάζειν are written together—1 Thess 2:12 and 2 Thess 1:3—only in these verses of Paul's letters.

2 Thess	1 Thess
2.1–12	a) 4.14–17
1 Ἐρωτῶμεν δὲ ὑμᾶς, ἀδελφοί, ὑπὲρ τῆς παρουσίας τοῦ κυρίου ἡμῶν Ἰησοῦ Χριστοῦ καὶ ἡμῶν ἐπισυναγωγῆς ἐπ' αὐτόν, 2 εἰς τὸ μὴ ταχέως σαλευθῆναι ὑμᾶς ἀπὸ τοῦ νοός κτλ.	14 ... ὁ θεὸς τοὺς κοιμηθέντας διὰ τοῦ Ἰησοῦ ἄξει σὺν αὐτῷ. 15 ... ἡμεῖς οἱ ζῶντες οἱ περιλειπόμενοι εἰς τὴν παρουσίαν τοῦ κυρίου οὐ μὴ φθάσωμεν ... 17 ... ἁρπαγησόμεθα ἐν νεφέλαις εἰς ἀπάντησιν τοῦ κυρίου.
	b) 5.12 (cf 4.1)
	ἐρωτῶμεν δὲ ὑμᾶς, ἀδελφοί ...

The introductory phrase, Ἐρωτῶμεν κτλ, is found in this form only in the letters to the Thessalonians. Cf. however Phil 4:3 ἐρωτῶ καὶ σέ.

In the entire first letter no counterparts can be found for the verses 2–12 of the second chapter of the second letter. These verses can therefore be omitted here. Nevertheless the following is worthy of note:

2 Thess	1 Thess
2.5	3.4
5 Οὐ μνημονεύετε, ὅτι ἔτι ὢν πρὸς ὑμᾶς ταῦτα ἔλεγον ὑμῖν;	καὶ γὰρ ὅτε πρὸς ὑμᾶς ἦμεν, προελέγομεν ὑμῖν ...

A μνημονεύετε with reference to the presence of Paul in Thessalonica is found in 1 Thess 2:9. A retrospective account of a visit with the readers in combination with ἔλεγον (προελέγομεν) ὑμῖν is not to be found again in any of Paul's other letters. Cf. also 2 Thess 3:10.

---

3. I make similar notes also in those instances even where they do not mean much as with this example. The references that I add in relation to the overview will be amended at a later time.

2 Thess	1 Thess
2.13–14	a) 2.12–13
13 Ἡμεῖς (a) δὲ ὀφείλομεν <u>εὐχαριστεῖν τῷ θεῷ</u> (a,b) <u>πάντοτε περὶ ὑμῶν</u> (b), <u>ἀδελφοὶ ἠγαπημένοι ὑπὸ κυρίου, ὅτι εἵλατο ὑμᾶς</u> (b cf d) ὁ <u>θεὸς</u> ἀπ' ἀρχῆς <u>εἰς σωτηρίαν</u> (d) <u>ἐν ἁγιασμῷ</u> (c) πνεύματος καὶ πίστει ἀληθείας, 14 εἰς ὃ ἐκάλεσεν (a,c) ὑμᾶς διὰ τοῦ εὐαγγελίου ἡμῶν <u>εἰς περιποίησιν</u> (d) <u>δόξης</u> (d,a) <u>τοῦ κυρίου</u> ἡμῶν Ἰησοῦ Χριστοῦ. (d)	12 . . . μαρτυρόμενοι εἰς τὸ περιπατεῖν ὑμᾶς ἀξίως <u>τοῦ θεοῦ τοῦ καλοῦντος</u> ὑμᾶς εἰς τὴν ἑαυτοῦ βασιλείαν καὶ <u>δόξαν</u>. 13 καὶ διὰ τοῦτο καὶ <u>ἡμεῖς εὐχαριστοῦμεν τῷ</u> θεῷ ἀδιαλείπτως, ὅτι . . . b) 1.2–4 2 <u>Εὐχαριστοῦμεν τῷ θεῷ πάντοτε περὶ</u> πάντων <u>ὑμῶν</u> . . . 4 εἰδότες, <u>ἀδελφοὶ ἠγαπημένοι ὑπὸ [τοῦ] θεοῦ, τὴν ἐκλογὴν ὑμῶν</u> . . . c) 4.7 οὐ γὰρ <u>ἐκάλεσεν</u> ἡμᾶς <u>ὁ θεὸς</u> ἐπὶ ἀκαθαρσίᾳ, ἀλλ' <u>ἐν ἁγιασμῷ</u>. d) 5.9 ὅτι οὐκ <u>ἔθετο</u> ἡμᾶς <u>ὁ θεὸς</u> εἰς ὀργήν, ἀλλὰ <u>εἰς περιποίησιν σωτηρίας διὰ τοῦ κυρίου ἡμῶν Ἰησοῦ Χριστοῦ</u>.

Here, at first sight, the parallels listed under b) and d) are the most striking and conspicuous. Apart from the fact that 1 Thess 1:2–4 with its phrase of thanksgiving, the thought and contemplation of Divine Election, and the phrase ἀδελφοὶ ἠγαπημένοι ὑπὸ τοῦ θεοῦ (2 Thess: ὑπὸ κυρίου) are exactly similar to the other letter, it is striking and noteworthy that this phrase of Paul's is found only in the letters to the Thessalonians (Rom 1:7: ἀγαπητοὶ θεοῦ).[4] The same can be said for περιποίησιν (see d). (Cf. however Eph 1:14, etc.) 1 Thess 5:9 can be compared not only to 2 Thess 2:14, but also to the preceding verse with its εἵλατο ὑμᾶς ὁ θεὸς εἰς σωτηρίαν.

---

4. Deut 33:12 of the LXX reads as follows: Benjamin ἠγαπημένος ὑπὸ κυρίου.

2 Thess	1 Thess
2.15–3.5[A]	a) to verse. 17:
15 Ἄρα οὖν, ἀδελφοί, <u>στήκετε</u> καὶ κρατεῖτε <u>τὰς παραδόσεις ἃς ἐδιδάχθητε</u> (see I 4.1) εἴτε διὰ λόγου εἴτε δι' ἐπιστολῆς <u>ἡμῶν</u>. 16 <u>Αὐτὸς δὲ ὁ κύριος ἡμῶν Ἰησοῦς Χριστὸς καὶ ὁ θεὸς ὁ πατὴρ ἡμῶν</u>, ὁ ἀγαπήσας ἡμᾶς καὶ δοὺς παράκλησιν αἰωνίαν καὶ ἐλπίδα ἀγαθὴν ἐν χάριτι, 17 <u>παρακαλέσαι ὑμῶν τὰς καρδίας</u> καὶ <u>στηρίξαι</u> (a, b) ἐν παντὶ ἔργῳ καὶ λόγῳ ἀγαθῷ. 3.1 Τὸ <u>λοιπὸν προσεύχεσθε, ἀδελφοί, περὶ ἡμῶν,</u> (c) ἵνα ὁ λόγος τοῦ κυρίου τρέχῃ καὶ δοξάζηται καθὼς καὶ πρὸς ὑμᾶς, 2 καὶ ἵνα ῥυσθῶμεν ἀπὸ τῶν ἀτόπων καὶ πονηρῶν ἀνθρώπων· οὐ γὰρ πάντων ἡ πίστις. 3 <u>Πιστὸς</u> δέ ἐστιν <u>ὁ κύριος</u>, ὃς (c) στηρίξει ὑμᾶς καὶ φυλάξει ἀπὸ τοῦ πονηροῦ. 4 πεποίθαμεν δὲ ἐν κυρίῳ ἐφ' ὑμᾶς, ὅτι <u>ἃ παραγγέλλομεν</u> [καὶ] ποιεῖτε καὶ ποιήσετε. 5 Ὁ δὲ <u>κύριος κατευθύναι ὑμῶν τὰς καρδίας</u> εἰς τὴν ἀγάπην τοῦ θεοῦ καὶ εἰς τὴν ὑπομονὴν τοῦ Χριστοῦ.	3.2 ... εἰς τὸ <u>στηρίξαι</u> ὑμᾶς καὶ <u>παρακαλέσαι</u> ... b) 3.8–4.2 8 ὅτι νῦν ζῶμεν, ἐὰν ὑμεῖς στήκετε ἐν κυρίῳ. ... 11 <u>Αὐτὸς δὲ ὁ θεὸς καὶ πατὴρ ἡμῶν καὶ ὁ κύριος ἡμῶν Ἰησοῦς κατευθύναι</u> τὴν ὁδὸν ἡμῶν πρὸς ὑμᾶς· 12 ὑμᾶς δὲ ὁ κύριος πλεονάσαι καὶ περισσεύσαι τῇ ἀγάπῃ εἰς ἀλλήλους καὶ εἰς πάντας, καθάπερ καὶ ἡμεῖς εἰς ὑμᾶς, 13 εἰς τὸ <u>στηρίξαι ὑμῶν τὰς καρδίας</u> ἀμέμπτους ἐν ἁγιωσύνῃ ἔμπροσθεν τοῦ θεοῦ καὶ πατρὸς ἡμῶν ἐν τῇ παρουσίᾳ ... 4.1 <u>Λοιπὸν</u> οὖν, ἀδελφοί, ἐρωτῶμεν ὑμᾶς ..., ἵνα <u>καθὼς παρελάβετε παρ' ἡμῶν</u> τὸ πῶς δεῖ ὑμᾶς περιπατεῖν ... 2 οἴδατε γὰρ τίνας <u>παραγγελίας ἐδώκαμεν ὑμῖν</u> ... c) to 4.1–3: 5.24–25 24 <u>πιστὸς ὁ καλῶν ὑμᾶς</u>, ὃς καὶ ποιήσει. 25 Ἀδελφοί. <u>προσεύχεσθε περὶ ἡμῶν</u>.

A. We add here 2 Thess 3:1 ff. so that all that reminds us of 1 Thess 3:8—4:2 will be placed side by side.

The request for intercession for the apostle (see c) can also be found with Col 4:3 (προσευχόμενοι ἅμα καὶ περὶ ἡμῶν). The congruence and similarity in wording of the two passages above may be noted with regard to one another; each time the imperative is employed and each time the word ἀδελφοί is used. Passages such as Rom 15:20, Phil 1:19, Phlm 22, and 2 Cor 1:11 are further differentiated from this wording. Cf. however Heb 13:18: Πιστὸς ὁ θεός (2 Thess: ὁ κύριος) ὅς (δι' οὗ ...) and also 1 Cor 10:13, 1: 9 (cf. 2 Cor 1:18).

The word, κατευθύνειν, is not to be found again in any other of Paul's writings outside of the two letters to the Thessalonians; elsewhere it is found in the New Testament only in Luke 1:79, although it is found not seldom in the apocryphal texts, cf. for example Sir 29:17; 39:7; 49:2–3; 51:20. With regard to 2 Thess 3:5 and 1 Thess 3:11, we find each time the same optative, κατευθῦναι; however, the meaning is different insofar as the objects are different (1 Thess: τὴν ὁδόν; 2 Thess: τὰς καρδίας). But that does not signify anything at all against the possibility of literary dependence here. The fact that a writer who uses a previous text records a word despite a difference of meaning is not a seldom occurrence. Whoever, for example, holds the view that Jas 4:6–10 is dependent on 1 Pet 5:5–9 (or the opposite) will not doubt that the word ὑποτάγητε (1 Pet 5:5 or Jas 4:7) also comes from the original text, although in the First Letter of Peter obedience to the πρεσβύτεροι is called for, whereas in the Letter of James obedience to God is demanded.

2 Thess	1 Thess
3.6–15	a) to verse. 6f, 10–12; 4.1f, 10f
6 Παραγγέλλομεν δὲ ὑμῖν, ἀδελφοί, ἐν ὀνόματι τοῦ κυρίου [ἡμῶν] Ἰησοῦ Χριστοῦ, στέλλεσθαι ὑμᾶς ἀπὸ παντὸς ἀδελφοῦ ἀτάκτως (e) περιπατοῦντος καὶ μὴ κατὰ τὴν παράδοσιν ἣν παρελάβοσαν παρ᾽ ἡμῶν. 7 αὐτοὶ γὰρ οἴδατε πῶς δεῖ μιμεῖσθαι ἡμᾶς, (c) ὅτι οὐκ ἠτακτήσαμεν (e) ἐν ὑμῖν, 8 οὐδὲ δωρεὰν ἄρτον ἐφάγομεν παρά τινος, ἀλλ᾽ ἐν κόπῳ καὶ μόχθῳ νυκτὸς καὶ ἡμέρας ἐργαζόμενοι πρὸς τὸ μὴ ἐπιβαρῆσαί τινα ὑμῶν (b)· 9 οὐχ ὅτι οὐκ ἔχομεν ἐξουσίαν, ἀλλ᾽ ἵνα ἑαυτοὺς τύπον (c) δῶμεν ὑμῖν εἰς τὸ μιμεῖσθαι ἡμᾶς (c). 10 καὶ γὰρ ὅτε ἦμεν πρὸς ὑμᾶς (d), τοῦτο παρηγγέλλομεν ὑμῖν, ὅτι εἴ τις οὐ θέλει ἐργάζεσθαι, μηδὲ ἐσθιέτω. 11 ἀκούομεν γάρ τινας περιπατοῦντας ἐν ὑμῖν ἀτάκτως, μηδὲν ἐργαζομένους ἀλλὰ περιεργαζομένους· 12 τοῖς δὲ τοιούτοις παραγγέλλομεν καὶ παρακαλοῦμεν ἐν κυρίῳ Ἰησοῦ Χριστῷ ἵνα μετὰ ἡσυχίας ἐργαζόμενοι τὸν ἑαυτῶν ἄρτον ἐσθίωσιν. 13 Ὑμεῖς δέ, ἀδελφοί, μὴ ἐγκακήσητε καλοποιοῦντες. 14 εἰ δέ τις οὐχ ὑπακούει τῷ λόγῳ ἡμῶν διὰ τῆς ἐπιστολῆς, τοῦτον σημειοῦσθε, μὴ συναναμίγνυσθαι αὐτῷ, ἵνα ἐντραπῇ· 15 καὶ μὴ ὡς ἐχθρὸν ἡγεῖσθε, ἀλλὰ νουθετεῖτε ὡς ἀδελφόν.	4.1 Λοιπὸν οὖν, ἀδελφοί, ἐρωτῶμεν ὑμᾶς καὶ παρακαλοῦμεν ἐν κυρίῳ Ἰησοῦ, ἵνα καθὼς παρελάβετε παρ᾽ ἡμῶν τὸ πῶς δεῖ ὑμᾶς περιπατεῖν καὶ ἀρέσκειν θεῷ καθὼς καὶ περιπατεῖτε, ἵνα περισσεύητε μᾶλλον. 2 οἴδατε γὰρ τίνας παραγγελίας ἐδώκαμεν ὑμῖν διὰ τοῦ κυρίου Ἰησοῦ . . . 10 . . . Παρακαλοῦμεν δὲ ὑμᾶς, ἀδελφοί, περισσεύειν μᾶλλον 11 καὶ φιλοτιμεῖσθαι ἡσυχάζειν καὶ πράσσειν τὰ ἴδια καὶ ἐργάζεσθαι ταῖς χερσὶν ὑμῶν, καθὼς ὑμῖν παρηγγείλαμεν, ἵνα περιπατῆτε εὐσχημόνως. . . Compare verse 7 with 2.1 αὐτοὶ γὰρ οἴδατε . . . b) to verse 8: 2:9 μνημονεύετε γάρ, ἀδελφοί, τὸν κόπον ἡμῶν καὶ τὸν μόχθον· νυκτὸς καὶ ἡμέρας ἐργαζόμενοι πρὸς τὸ μὴ ἐπιβαρῆσαί τινα ὑμῶν ἐκηρύξαμεν . . . c) to verse 7, 9: 1.6–7 6 καὶ ὑμεῖς μιμηταὶ ἡμῶν ἐγενήθητε καὶ τοῦ κυρίου, δεξάμενοι τὸν λόγον ἐν θλίψει πολλῇ, μετὰ χαρᾶς πνεύματος ἁγίου, 7 ὥστε γενέσθαι ὑμᾶς τύπον πᾶσιν τοῖς πιστεύουσιν . . .

	d) to verse 9:
	3.4
	4 <u>καὶ γὰρ ὅτε πρὸς ὑμᾶς ἦμεν</u> . . .
	e) to verse 6f, 11, 15:
	5.13–14
	13 καὶ <u>ἡγεῖσθαι</u> αὐτοὺς (the presiders) ὑπερεκπερισσῶς <u>ἐν ἀγάπῃ</u> . . . εἰρηνεύετε ἐν ἑαυτοῖς. 14 Παρακαλοῦμεν δὲ ὑμᾶς, ἀδελφοί, <u>νουθετεῖτε τοὺς ἀτάκτους</u>.

For the word, ἀτάκτως (2 Thess 3:6, 11, cf. 2 Thess 3:7, ἀτακτεῖν), it should be mentioned that this word only occurs in the New Testament in 1 Thess 5:14, though admittedly as an adjective.

I have listed and set apart the word, τὸν ἑαυτῶν ἄρτον (2 Thess 3:12), because it could well have been prompted by τὰ ἴδια (1 Thess 4:11).

The phrase, μὴ ὡς ἐχθρὸν ἡγεῖσθε (2 Thess 3:15), can very possibly be an equivalent of ἡγεῖσθαι ἐν ἀγάπῃ despite the relationship to totally different people.

2 Thess	1 Thess
3.16–18	5.23, 28
16 <u>Αὐτὸς δὲ ὁ κύριος τῆς εἰρήνης</u> δῴη ὑμῖν τὴν εἰρήνην διὰ παντὸς ἐν παντὶ τρόπῳ. ὁ κύριος μετὰ πάντων ὑμῶν. 17 Ὁ ἀσπασμὸς τῇ ἐμῇ χειρὶ Παύλου, ὅ ἐστιν σημεῖον ἐν πάσῃ ἐπιστολῇ· οὕτως γράφω. 18 <u>ἡ χάρις τοῦ κυρίου ἡμῶν Ἰησοῦ Χριστοῦ μετὰ πάντων ὑμῶν.</u>	23 <u>Αὐτὸς δὲ ὁ θεὸς τῆς εἰρήνης</u> ἁγιάσαι ὑμᾶς ὁλοτελεῖς . . . 28 <u>Ἡ χάρις τοῦ κυρίου ἡμῶν Ἰησοῦ Χριστοῦ μεθ' ὑμῶν.</u>

This last sentence is found regularly in the same or an expanded form in the closing of Paul's letters. Cf. Rom 16:20; 1 Cor 16:23, etc.

In the present comparative overview the same passages of the first letter are repeatedly cited several times. This requires no special justification. A repeated dependence of the same passage is just as possible as the use of different passages of the original text for one single dependent composition or writing.

Furthermore, it must be emphasized from the outset that this listed comparative material has many different meanings. Even if evidence of the use of the first letter for the second letter has been provided, the extent of the dependence in specific points will never be able to be determined with certainty. If the word, νουθετεῖτε, of 2 Thess 3:15 should have been prompted by 1 Thess 5:14, so nonetheless the phrase next to it, μὴ ὡς ἐχθρὸν ἡγεῖσθε, does not have to have anything to do with the phrase, ἡγεῖσθαι ἐν ἀγάπῃ (1 Thess 5:18). If the passage of 2 Thess 3:6 should actually rest upon 1 Thess 4:1, so it is not yet at all without doubt that the words, οἴδατε and πῶς δεῖ from 2 Thess 3:7, have been derived from the words, οἴδατε of 1 Thess 4:2 and πῶς δεῖ from 1 Thess 4:1. Although the word, τύπος (1 Thess 1:7), occurs in close proximity to the words, μιμηταὶ ἡμῶν (1 Thess 1:6), τύπος right next to μιμεῖσθαι ἡμᾶς in the second letter is by no means a definite remembrance of that particular passage. Not simply because there τύπος is engaged by the readers and here it is said and written by Paul, but also because always wherever μιμεῖσθαι is mentioned τύπος is found next to or near it. Yet it is not at all necessary that μιμεῖσθαι ἡμᾶς be determined by μιμηταὶ ἡμῶν that occurs in another context. As soon as the author of the second letter made the work of the apostle Paul actually the ideal example for the idle ones, so the word, μιμεῖσθαι, came to be used easily enough on its own. Similar explanations and assessments can be made for many other cases. On the contrary, an influence of the original text can exist with regard to the actual literary relationship between letters, whereas for two arbitrary letters no one would think about or consider this. Therefore, we could not exclude such cases and situations from our survey; at most we have been able to omit some few especially doubtful ones. It was just as unlikely and impossible at the outset to undertake a division of the parallels according to the categories of "important" and "not important."

The relationship of the two letters to the Thessalonians is in some ways obviously different from the relatedness which we can observe between other letters of the early Christian period. The relationship of the Letter of James to the First Letter of Peter, that of the Second Letter of Peter to the Letter of Jude, that of the Letter of Polycarp to the First Letter of Peter or to the First Letter of Clement offer no real and actual analogy. Somewhat more likely is the relationship between the Letter to the Ephesians and the Letter to the Colossians, but nevertheless only to a very limited extent.

The related parallels in the second letter do not just appear with certain single points of contact, rather they pervade the entire letter. Only the eschatological section of 2 Thess 2:2–12 offers an exception which immediately stands out.

Exact verbal repetitions for only isolated specific verses and passages are not found very often. Rather the parallels to the text of the first letter are most often scattered over larger sections of the second letter. For this reason one does not have the impression that the first letter has, in an exact and strict sense, been simply written out and copied.

Usually a definite passage from the first letter provides the parallels for most of the sections. Then too other passages and situations offer themselves, as it often happens, with no little exigency for comparison. The comparative words and verbal usages of the first letter thus appear to emerge in a colorful sequence throughout the text of the second letter. Thus the entire relationship of the correspondence and similarity of the two gives to a certain extent the impression of complexity and obscurity.

Elsewhere, furthermore, the exact similarity of single expressions, significant concepts, thoughts and thought-combinations often impose upon us most emphatically the assumption of a relationship of dependency. Only very seldom, however, is exact similarity presented to us, which admittedly with regard to the entire character of the letters to the Thessalonians again does not astound us. Rather in contrast to that, so much greater is the correspondence and agreement of expressions, verbal usages, phrases, such as we would easily trust and expect of Paul with his very different occasions of address and admonition.

Assuredly this is to some extent to be ascribed to the facts, whereby the entire relationship of the two letters has made no definite impression upon very impartial and unbiased scholars. Meanwhile the mere list of comparisons should nevertheless perplex and confound such scholars, even before one looks closer at the list of parallels.

Above all, the rather consistent large quantity of the many contacts between the two letters is immediately evident. Without a special explanation the quantity of them remains incomprehensible. For the most part, one can of course rather easily and with little deliberation determine the meaning of some of the parallels. But here they should be acknowledged in their entirety. At any rate, there are more parallels to the first letter in the short second letter to the Thessalonians than there are in all of Paul's letters and certainly in all of the written documents of the New Testament combined.[5] Furthermore, among all of Paul's letters—I do not consider the Letter to the Ephesians to be one of them—a similar relationship of related-

---

5. Cf. Holtzmann, "Zum zweiten Thessalonicherbrief," 106; *Schenkels Bibellexikon*, 509.

ness does not occur for a second time. In the Letter to the Galatians and in the Letter to the Romans, for example, we do certainly find various parallels of expression and thought among those passages where related themes are dealt with. Nevertheless, there with those passages we never have the impression of a repetition as here, because assuredly the similarity seems to disappear when some different aspects emerge. Moreover, there the parallels are to be explained without exception from the property and acquirement of definite theological thoughts and teachings or firm and practical principles. This may also be reminiscent of the letters of Ignatius. Who will thus find among the letters mentioned above only one reasonable analogy for our study? Certainly something remarkably different is evident here.

But the similarity of the two letters to the Thessalonians extends substantially further than the first impression allows one to recognize and appreciate. The texual evidence which is to be explained here is not at all to be denoted and described with the simple overview of the parallels. The overview must be interpreted and completed by means of many other factors and elements which are not depicted from the overview alone.

1) That meager amount of information that allows itself to be ascertained and established from the second letter with regard to the presupposed historical situation coincides and overlaps in essence with the details from the first letter.

Silvanus and Timothy are here as also in the first letter with the Apostle (1 Thess 1:1; 2 Thess 1:1). The state of the Christian life in Thessalonica is generally pleasantly gratifying (1 Thess 1:3–8; 2 Thess 1:3–7). Nonetheless many of the community are to be reproached for their disturbed and disorderly character and idleness (1 Thess 4:10–13; 5:14; 2 Thess 3:6–15). According to each letter questions concerning the hope for the future sway and stir up the community. Each letter speaks of persecution and affliction for these Christians (1 Thess 1:6; 2:14; 3:3–7; 2 Thess 1:4–7). Furthermore, everything which could perhaps appear to be new in the second letter occurs at all events within this common framework. At most only the mention of the ἄτοποι and the πονηροὶ ἄνθρωποι of 2 Thess 3:2 goes over and beyond this. But this statement is at first very unclear and out of context, especially if these people appear to be at that place from which Paul was writing.

One has now understood from this letter that since the sending of the first letter, a new persecution has come upon the community under which vehemence the quixotic tumult and idleness have grown far beyond their earlier extent.⁶ The general possibility of such a series of events I do not dispute or challenge. Yet first of all if actually it is simply this sequence, that the persecution is the cause of the clamor and tumult and idleness, then the letter itself does not hint at or even imply this with one word. But it is not even certain that the first letter—with its expression ἐπάθετε (1 Thess 2:14)—establishes the earlier persecution as a past event.⁷ The second letter namely speaks without doubt of the present tribulation but does not distinguish this as something new.

If the neglect of daily work is to be viewed as the consequence of clamorous hope for the future, as for the most part one assumes, so also that impatient faith and belief in the nearness of the Day of the Lord, of which 2 Thess 2:1–12 speaks, would not lead to anything beyond the first letter. Yet one would only be tempted to conclude from the harsh tone of the second letter that the impulsive clamor and neglect of work have escalated considerably since the earlier letter. But once more that has not been stated here. Incidentally, the questions still remains open as to whether or not the reprehensible idleness is related to the tumultuous eschatological excitement. At any rate the one single, definite reference to tangible events is contained in 2 Thess 2:2, the one reference which could have occurred since the sending of the first letter. We learn there that an arousing, exceptional excitement has taken hold; and that in this eschatological fever certain pneumatic manifestations and meetings of the community along with written letters as well as oral statements of the Apostle have played some kind of role, be they only putative, perhaps even forced or foisted, or actually real. Aside from this one could only further refer and point to the extremely "barren" declaration that Paul has received news from Thessalonica (ἀκούομεν 2 Thess 3:11).

We also encounter meager historical content in our letter, such that it is rather doubtful that 2 Thess 2:2 can at all be explained. Nowhere are positive facts, names, events, or situations given, which thus presents difficulties for the assumption for the inauthenticity of the letter because the fabrication of them would be psychologically incomprehensible.⁸

First of all, it does not depend just on the negative, but rather much more upon the evidence that the parallelism of the two letters based on

---

6. Cf. Klöpper, "Der 2 Brief an die Thessalonicher," 86ff.

7. Cf. 2 Thess 3:8; Bornemann, *DieThessalonicherbriefe*, 334; Zahn, *Einleitung*, 158; Hofmann, *Die heiligen Schrift*, I:2, 366.

8. Cf. Zahn, *Ignatius von Antiochien*, 540–41; *Einleitung* I, 113–14.

the documented aspects and standpoints is already strange and unusual. Admittedly one can say with some justification that substantially altered developments in the community in Thessalonica do not at all allow themselves to be anticipated a short time after the writing of the first letter. Yet for all that it is against the expectation that one of Paul's letters, even also when it followed so soon after an earlier one, mentions so very little about the events which in the meantime would have taken place. Even there where he really should allude and refer to such, nowhere at all does he comment that since the earlier time an event or change has occurred. But it is no less noteworthy, as it appears to me, that nowhere at all does he allow matters to be highlighted that the first letter could already have mentioned but that coincidentally are not mentioned. For it is obvious that the first letter does not give us a complete description of the life of the community and the events in Thessalonica that had significance and importance for Paul.

2) The result is similar when one compares the two letters according to their *content of thoughts*. Once more with the exception of the pericope about the Anti-Christ, our letter presents basically only thoughts which nevertheless were also developed or touched on in the first letter. It is gratuitous to demonstrate that more closely. The requirement and demand for ecclesiastical rule and behavior (2 Thess 3:6, 12–15) one could well distinguish as a unique element of the second letter.[9] However because it is only mentioned with regard to the ἄτακτοι, it deals here merely with a modification of the realization and development of the theme of 1 Thess 4:10–13. It is similar to the passage 2 Thess 1:5–9, the mention of the court of retribution for those who badger and pester the community. The origin and source for this small digression, the concept of θλῖψις, is to be found also in the first letter (1 Thess 1:6).[10] Even the Apocalypse passage, 2 Thess 2:1–12 by the way, is found as *a teaching about the time of the Parousia* (2 Thess 2:2) under a viewpoint which is found once more in the eschatological section of the first letter. The second part of this theme is actually valid for the question about the χρόνοι and the καιροί (1 Thess 5:1). Thus the entire second letter does not actually offer a new theme at all.

3) Closely related to that stated above under number 2 but yet especially emphasized here is the fact that the *structure and arrangement* of the second letter corresponds remarkably to that of the first letter.[11]

---

9. Cf. Bornemann, *Die Thessalonicherbriefe*, 481.
10. I refrain from any consideration of 1 Thess 2:14–16.
11. Cf. especially Weizsäcker's appropriate comments: Weizsäcker, *Das Apostolische*

Still not all sections of the first letter have an equivalent in the second. Most notably the passage 1 Thess 2:1–16 as well as that of 1 Thess 2:17—3:10 remain entirely without any equivalent. Yet conversely one can place *each section of the second letter alongside a section with similar and related content from the first letter.* The first passage presents each time thanksgiving for the inner thriving and prosperity of the community. An eschatological section in the first letter, 1 Thess 4:15—5:5, is also related to the second passage in the second letter, 2 Thess 2:1–12. The section 2 Thess 2:15—3: 5, which in its wish and admonition speaks excellently of the steadfastness of the readers and of their abiding with the received, apostolic teaching, corresponds to 1 Thess 3:11—4:8 and is to be placed more precisely alongside the first part of this section to 1 Thess 4:2. Last of all follows the warning of idleness that comprises 2 Thess 3:6–15 which corresponds to 1Thess 4:10-12. The objection that each section according to the related length and style of the composition demonstrates a great diverseness cannot alone refute the perception and conclusion stated above. If the eschatological passage stood at the very end of the letter, then the sequence of the sections would unfold according to the same order of the first letter.

4) Although at first the relatedness of the two letters appears to be complicated,[12] the fact results easily from closer observation and consideration *that the specific contacts for the most part present themselves in corresponding passages of the letters, namely within the identified parallel sections.* When thus numerous or even diverse details and particulars from one passage of the first letter have their equivalent in the second letter, so these details do not appear in small isolated parts as though they were randomly distributed throughout the entire letter, but they occur rather as a rule combined in relationships between single, small textual units.[13] This

---

Zeitalter, 249–50, 259–60. Cf. Zahn, *Einleitung*, 160, 174. He emphasizes the similarity of the structure of the two letters.

Cf. Holtzmann, "Zum zweiten Thessalonicherbrief," 104.

12. Cf. the text above from 9–12.

13. The impression that one attains of this relatedness is somewhat different depending upon the perspective as to whether or not one searches for possible parallels from the first letter for texts of the second letter or conversely for parallels from the second letter that are related to passages of the first letter. The critical scholar will not neglect this aspect, but the comparison is dependent upon the latter. The reason for this lies with the fact that there are many parallels from the second letter that are distinctly related to passages of the first letter that actually form a "spillover" of passages for the second letter, while on the contrary passages from the second letter do not determine the content of the first letter.

fact deserves the utmost attention. It seems to me that it is the fault of biblical criticism that it has not actually made this clear.

Although the particular has already allowed itself to be gathered and extracted from the earlier comparison of the texts, I want to present and show the primary characteristics here quickly in a chart about which there can be no doubt because of the much easier orientation. It will be sufficient to write out the parallel words.

Of those usages and words that actually have parallels, their counterparts can be found.

II 1.3–12	in the first letter
Εὐχαριστεῖν—τῷ θεῷ πάντοτε περὶ ὑμῶν—ἡ πίστις—ἡ ἀγάπη—the motif of praising, verse 4—τῆς ὑπομονῆς—πίστεως—θλίψεσιν—πᾶσιν τοῖς πιστεύσασιν (?) προσευχόμεθα πάντοτε περὶ ὑμῶν—ἔργον πίστεως.	I 1.2–8
2.15–3.5	3.11 (8)—4.2
στήκετε (I 3.8)—τὰς παραδόσεις ἃς ἐδιδάχθητε (I 4.1)—αὐτὸς δὲ ὁ κύριος ἡμῶν Ἰησοῦς Χριστὸς καὶ ὁ θεὸς ὁ πατὴρ ἡμῶν—ὑμῶν τὰς καρδίας—στηρίξαι—τὸ λοιπόν—ἃ παραγγέλλομεν—κατευθύναι—ὑμῶν τὰς καρδίας.	
3.6–12	4.1–12
Παραγγέλλομεν ὑμῖν, ἀδελφοί, ἐν (ὀνόματι τοῦ) κυρίου Ἰησοῦ—περιπατοῦντος—κατὰ τὴν παράδοσιν ἣν παρελάβοσαν παρ' ἡμῶν—γὰρ οἴδατε—πῶς δεῖ—παρηγγέλλομεν (the past tense) ὑμῖν—ἐργάζεσθαι—παραγγέλλομεν καὶ παρακαλοῦμεν ἐν κυρίῳ Ἰησοῦ Χριστῷ—μετὰ ἡσυχίας ἐργαζόμενοι—[τὸν] ἑαυτῶν [ἄρτον] (?)	But 4.3–9 does not come into question here, but in truth 4.1- 2, 10–12 does. 1 Thess 4.1–2 and 2 Thess 3.6–7, also 1 Thess 4.10–12 and 2 Thess 3.10–12 correspond with each other.
3.1–3	
προσεύχεσθε, ἀδελφοί, περὶ ἡμῶν—πιστὸς δέ ἐστιν ὁ κύριος, ὅς . . .	5.24–25

Over and against the definite cluster of parallels found in small, single sections of the first letter, that which in the second letter reminds us and refers to other sections of the first letter clearly recedes somewhat into the background, just as those parallels that remind us of these similar ones are nonetheless on the contrary dispersed throughout the highlighted parallelism of the chapters.[14] However that may be, one cannot deny that these corresponding parallels at specific places in the text of the one and then the other letter definitely require an explanation. It would be another matter if one dealt only with expressions that arose on their own with the discussion of specific themes (as ἐργάζεσθαι, when one speaks of idleness). The truth is that one is dealing here with completely neutral usages and phrases.

5) An additional correlation to that which has been presented above lies in the fact that in very many cases *single parallels occur at places (especially insertions in the text of the letter) that match one another remarkably.*

a) In both of these letters the theme of thanksgiving of the greeting is directly taken up once more, 1 Thess 2:13 and 2 Thess 2:13. That does not otherwise occur in any of Paul's letters.[15] The subject of the thanksgiving is thereby especially emphasized in both passages by the use of ἡμεῖς. This could be mere coincidence, but it thus first of all attracts our attention because such a ἡμεῖς (ἐγώ) is not found in our letters and not in one of any other of Paul's letters in the thanksgiving of the greeting. The passages in which the thanksgiving appears for a second time may for that matter be compared to one another.[16] The complete section 2 Thess 2:1–12 presents something new in contrast to the same section of the first letter. On the other hand the section 1 Thess 2:1–12, when the anticipatory expression is permitted here, is as a complete unit simply skipped over in the second letter. If one therefore disregards these two sections, thus an analogous and similar section unfolds. One may further add and surmise that the section which immediately follows upon 2 Thess 2:13–14 has its equivalent with verses 1 Thess 3:11–13, i.e., in the section of the first letter, which when we are again permitted to disregard the once "skipped over" section 1 Thess 2:17—3:10, follows upon 1 Thess 2:13–16, i.e., the position and passage of the second thanksgiving.[17]

---

14. For example 2 Thess 2:13 has a definite parallel in 1 Thess 1:4 etc.

15. 1 Cor 1:14 is certainly not comparable. Eph 1:16 is not a resumption of the theme of thanksgiving but mentions it here for the first time.

16. Cf. Schmiedel, Untitled Entry, *Handkommentar*, 8–10.

17. The following chart of these comparisons serves as an illustration of these explicated texts by means of a later implementation: a) 1 Thess 1:1–10 (1 Thess 2:1–12); 1 Thess 2:13, (16); (1 Thess 2:17—3:10); 1 Thess 3:11–13. b) 2 Thess 1:1–12 (2 Thess 2:1–12); 2 Thess 2:13, (14); 2 Thess 2:15–17 (resp. 2 Thess 3:5). Those verses which cannot be compared have been enclosed in parentheses.

The possibility that the one passage has been copied from the other is now rather substantially increased when one observes that the adjacent expression 2 Thess 2:14 ἐκάλεσεν ὑμᾶς ὁ θεός . . . εἰς περιποίησιν δόξης mirrors and reminds us of 1 Thess 2:12, and most specifically when one looks closer at the ἡμεῖς δὲ of 2 Thess 2:13. It is clear that 1 Thess 2:13 has been motivated by the use of the pronoun, for it forms the opposite in contrast to the Thessalonians, the readers.[18] Not only the Thessalonians will be thankful for the activity and successes of the Apostle; but although the matter here deals with his own action, he also—be that alone or with his helpers (καὶ ἡμεῖς)—will benefit from the blessing that this mission has had. In the second letter on the contrary the ἡμεῖς δὲ is at first redundant, for ὀφείλομεν δέ would mean exactly the same. But actually ἡμεῖς δὲ allows, as Schmiedel[19] has recognized, for an extreme opposite to emerge. Both of the successive following verses speak of the court of judgment for those who do not believe the truth. In contrast to these people stand now the readers whom God has not appointed for the judgment but rather has chosen for salvation.

Thus the sentence should perhaps read: εὐχαριστεῖν δὲ ὀφείλομεν τῷ θεῷ πάντοτε, ὅτι ὑμᾶς εἵλατο ὁ θεός . . . εἰς σωτηρίαν. Instead rather Paul either alone or together with Silvanus and Timothy steps forward by means of ἡμεῖς δέ to confront the unbelievers. If then ἡμεῖς has mechanically been taken from 1 Thess 2:13, so this provides the simplest explanation.[20]

b) and c) The usage αὐτὸς δὲ ὁ θεός (2 Thess: κύριος) with the following optative is found twice in both letters to the Thessalonians, and as also Schmiedel[21] has seen, both times at exactly corresponding places of the text. The first time it occurs at the beginning of a group of thoughts, the correspondence of which was referred to above, namely 2 Thess 2:16 and 1 Thess 3:11. The second time this usage is found after the conclusion of the admonitions at the beginning of the actual closing, specifically 2 Thess 3:16 and 1 Thess 5:23. A most striking and obvious parallelism!

18. Cf. Schmiedel, "Untitled Entry," *Handkommentar*; Bornemann, *Die Thessalonicherbriefe*.

19. Also Holtzmann, "Zum zweiten Thessalonicherfbrief," 101.

20. Von Hofmann denies that the community corresponds to the people to whom the verses 10–12 refer and describe because otherwise the ἡμεῖς δὲ cannot be understood. Therein lies indirectly the recognition of the difficulty, for it is rather unnatural to eliminate that oppostion. Bornemann has correctly determined the consequential relationship between v. 12 and v. 13, but does not provide a satisfactory explanation for the ἡμεῖς δέ.

21. Schmiedel, Untitled Entry, *Handkommentar*, 8–10.

To that may be added that an αὐτὸς δὲ ὁ θεός (κύριος) has never elsewhere been verified in Paul's writings.[22] Furthermore the optative of wish, with the exception of Paul's frequent use of μὴ γένοιτο, occurs also very seldom elsewhere in the New Testament. Only Rom 15:5, 13 allow for a comparison in the first of Paul's letters to the texts above (see also 2 Thess 3:5, resumption of 2 Thess 2:16).[23] Nonetheless a further perception allows the parallelism to appear even more parallel. The complete texts read as follows:

I	II
3.11: Αὐτὸς δὲ ὁ θεὸς καὶ πατὴρ ἡμῶν καὶ ὁ κύριος ἡμῶν Ἰησοῦς κατευθύναι . . .	2.16: Αὐτὸς δὲ ὁ κύριος ἡμῶν Ἰησοῦς Χριστὸς καὶ ὁ θεὸς ὁ πατὴρ ἡμῶν . . . παρακαλέσαι . . . (3.5: ὁ δὲ κύριος κατευθύναι . . .)
5.23 Αὐτὸς δὲ ὁ θεὸς τῆς εἰρήνης ἁγιάσαι . . .	3.16: Αὐτὸς δὲ ὁ κύριος τῆς εἰρήνης δῴη . . .

Thus that is to say the following: at first each time a complete form in which Christ is named alongside God, but God who is designated as θεὸς and πατήρ;[24] then secondly each time comes the addendum, τῆς εἰρήνης. Thereby the κατευθύναι of the first text is to be sure not found directly with 2 Thess 2:16, but on the contrary only a few verses later.[25] One can lessen and attenuate the meaning of the second text by means of the observation that ὁ θεὸς τῆς εἰρήνης tends to occur in Paul's letters exactly at closing passages.[26] Yet the remarkable aspect of the correspondence is thereby hardly minimized.

d) In the first letter after Paul has enunciated that wish just now mentioned in 1 Thess 3:11–13, he continues 1 Thess 4:1 with a λοιπὸν οὖν. With regard to the parallel wish of 2 Thess 2:16 a τὸ λοιπόν follows at its foot with the opening verse of 2 Thess 3:1. The immediate continuation is certainly different in both cases. Therefore the similarity does not need to arise from approximate relatedness, especially since τὸ λοιπόν (λοιπόν) is not at all

---

22. Cf. Burton, *Syntax of the Moods*, 79.

23. Cf. furthermore 2 Tim 1:16, 18; Heb 13:21.

24. Holzmann, "Zum zweiten Thessalonickerbrief," 101. Here he emphasizes that both times the subject God and Christ occurs, the predicate is rendered with the singular form.

25. Cf. above 7–9 for κατευθύνειν.

26. Cf. Rom 15:33; 16:20; 2 Cor 13:11; Phil 4:9; Heb 13:20.

often used as one of Paul's transitional words. Naturally as an isolated usage this has no meaning, but in relation with other examples it deserves to be mentioned.[27] It is similar to the following case.

e) Closely related with regard to their positions of occurrence are the texts 1 Thess 4:10b–12 and 2 Thess 3:10–12. Here it is worthy of note that precisely the same παραγγέλλειν appears each time in the praeteritum (1 Thess 4:11 παρηγγείλαμεν, 2 Thess 3:10 παρηγγέλλομεν), or that Paul with this same word is remembering his instruction which was given during his earlier visit. Παραγγέλλομεν (cf. also 2 Thess 3:6) occurs in Paul's letters with the exception of the Pastorals only two other times, namely in 1 Cor 7:10; 1 Cor 11:17.

f) The expressions which are found in the introduction of the eschatological section 2 Thess 2:1–12 (ὑπὲρ τῆς παρουσίας τοῦ κυρίου ἡμῶν Ἰησοῦ Χριστοῦ καὶ ἡμῶν ἐπισυναγωγῆς ἐπ'αὐτόν) are to be read as a retrospection of the beginning of the eschatological exposition of 1 Thess 4–5.[28] Also 1 Thess 4:15 speaks of the παρουσία τοῦ κυρίου, which Paul rarely ever mentions in his other letters. The expression, ἐπισυναγωγὴ ἐπ'αὐτόν, deserves considerably more attention. It occurs in the singular in Paul and it appears to be a summary, a concise hint of an expected event. We would hardly be able to interpret it with any certainty without the first letter. We understand the choice of expression when we read 1 Thess 4:14, ἄξει σὺν αὐτῷ; and then the expected event itself, however, when we accept and understand that 4:17 speaks of ἁρπάζεσθαι εἰς ἀπάντησιν τοῦ κυρίου εἰς ἀέρα.

6) When one comparatively follows the course and structure of both of the letters, it can be perceived that such provides the result *that a very important part of the parallelism arises in the exact same sequence.* May the reader forgive me when I present the chart once more. The most important aspect to be sure allows itself already to be gathered and understood from the remarks from numbers 3–5, but it is not superfluous to demonstrate once more especially the phenomenon as it unfolds.

The passages upon which everything depends have been underlined with straight lines. The parallels appear in regular print, and they crisscross and are scattered throughout the sequence of the related words. However, those parallels that are found only in a few different places, provided

---

27. Zahn, *Einleitung*, 160; Holtzmann, "Zum zweiten Thessalonicherbrief," 103. Zahn and Holtzmann have both recognized this similarity.

28. Here those scholars and exegetes who consider the letter to be of Pauline origin have often found a reference to the first letter.

that they at least belong to the sections and are parallel to the sequence, have been marked and underlined. With this comparison only a very few sections of the letter will be gathered together and considered. Within these excerpts the parallel words and usages appear exactly in the order in which they appear in the original text. Also I am listing here only the keywords, not the entire text; and I follow thereby the course and structure of the second letter. The chart takes into consideration those related contacts that are highlighted in the overview from pages 4 to 6.

2 Thess	1 Thess
1, 2 Παῦλος κτλ τῇ ἐκκλησίᾳ Θεσσαλονικέων ἐν θεῷ πατρὶ— καὶ κυρίῳ Ἰησοῦ Χριστῷ· χάρις κτλ.	1.1 Παῦλος κτλ τῇ ἐκκλησίᾳ Θεσσαλονικέων ἐν θεῷ πατρὶ καὶ κυρίῳ Ἰησοῦ Χριστῷ χάρις κτλ.
1.3 εὐχαριστεῖν—τῷ θεῷ πάντοτε περὶ ὑμῶν—ἡ πίστις	1.2,3 εὐχαριστοῦμεν τῷ θεῷ πάντοτε περὶ ὑμῶν—τῆς πίστεως
πλεονάζει ἡ ἀγάπη εἰς ἀλλήλους	τῆς ἀγάπης
	3.12 πλεονάσαι τῇ ἀγάπῃ εἰς ἀλλήλους
1.4 Praise of the Thessalonians among the communities.	1.7 The faith of the Thessalonians is well-known throughout the entire world.
	2.19 στέφανος καυχήσεως ἢ οὐχὶ καὶ ὑμεῖς
ἐν ταῖς ἐκκλησίαις τοῦ θεοῦ (?)	2.14 τῶν ἐκκλησιῶν τοῦ θεοῦ (?)
τῆς ὑπομονῆς—πίστεως—διωγμοῖς—θλίψεσιν	1.3 τῆς ὑπομονῆς
	1.6 ἐν θλίψει
	2.14 oppression
1.5 εἰς τὸ καταξιωθῆναι—τῆς βασιλείας τοῦ θεοῦ (see 1.11 ἀξιώσῃ τῆς κλήσεως)	2.12 περιπατεῖν ἀξίως τοῦ θεοῦ τοῦ καλοῦντος—βασιλείαν
1.7 ἐν τῇ ἀποκαλύψει τοῦ κυρίου Ἰησοῦ ἀπ' οὐρανοῦ μετ' ἀγγέλων αὐτοῦ	3.13 ἐν τῇ παρουσίᾳ τοῦ κυρίου—Ἰησοῦ μετὰ—τῶν ἁγίων αὐτοῦ
	4.16 ἀπ' οὐρανοῦ
1.8 ἐκδίκησιν—τοῖς μὴ εἰδόσιν θεόν	4.5-6 τὰ μὴ εἰδότα θεόν—ἔκδικος
1.10 ἐν τοῖς ἁγίοις αὐτοῦ	3.13 τῶν ἁγίων αὐτοῦ
1.10 ἐν πᾶσιν τοῖς πιστεύσασιν (?)	1.7 πᾶσιν τοῖς πιστεύουσιν (?)
1.11 προσευχόμεθα πάντοτε περὶ ὑμῶν	1.2 πάντοτε περὶ ὑμῶν τῶν προσευχῶν ἡμῶν
ἔργον πίστεως	1.3 ἔργον τῆς πίστεως

The Authenticity of the Second Letter to the Thessalonians

2.1 ἐρωτῶμεν δὲ ὑμᾶς, ἀδελφοί τῆς παρουσίας τοῦ κυρίου—ἡμῶν ἐπισυναγωγῆς ἐπ' αὐτόν	5.12 ἐρωτῶμεν δὲ ὑμᾶς, ἀδελφοί 4.14,15,17 ἄξει σὺν αὐτῷ—τὴν παρουσίαν τοῦ κυρίου—εἰς ἀπάντησιν
2.5 οὐ μνημονεύετε—ἔτι ὢν πρὸς ὑμᾶς—ἔλεγον ὑμῖν	3.4 ὅτε πρὸς ὑμᾶς ἤμεν. προελέγομεν ὑμῖν. (see 2.9 μνημονεύετε)
2.13-14 <u>ἡμεῖς—εὐχαριστεῖν τῷ θεῷ πάντοτε</u> περὶ ὑμῶν, ἀδελφοὶ ἠγαπημένοι ὑπὸ κυρίου—εἵλατο ὑμᾶς ὁ θεός—εἰς σωτηρίαν ἐν ἁγιασμῷ—<u>ἐκάλεσεν εἰς</u> περιποίησιν <u>δόξης</u> τοῦ κυρίου ἡμῶν Ἰησοῦ Χριστοῦ	2.12-13 <u>καλοῦντος—εἰς δόξαν—ἡμεῖς εὐχαριστοῦμεν τῷ θεῷ ἀδιαλείπτως</u> 1.2 εὐχαριστοῦμεν τῷ θεῷ πάντοτε περὶ ὑμῶν 1.4 ἀδελφοὶ ἠγαπημένοι ὑπὸ θεοῦ—τὴν ἐκλογήν 4.7 ἐκάλεσεν ὁ θεός—ἐν ἁγιασμῷ 5.9 ἔθετο ὁ θεός—εἰς περιποίησιν σωτηρίας τοῦ κυρίου ἡμῶν Ἰησοῦ Χριστοῦ
2.15 <u>στήκετε</u> <u>τὰς παραδόσεις, ἃς ἐδιδάχθητε—ἡμῶν</u> 2.16 <u>Αὐτὸς δὲ ὁ κύριος ἡμῶν Ἰησοῦς Χριστὸς καὶ ὁ θεὸς ὁ πατὴρ ἡμῶν—</u> 2.17 παρακαλέσαι <u>ὑμῶν τὰς καρδίας—</u>στηρίξαι (optional)	3.8 <u>στήκετε</u> 4.1 <u>καθὼς παρελάβετε παρ' ἡμῶν.</u> 3.11 <u>Αὐτὸς δὲ ὁ θεὸς καὶ πατὴρ ἡμῶν καὶ ὁ κύριος ἡμῶν Ἰησοῦς Χριστός—</u> 3.13 εἰς τὸ <u>στηρίξαι ὑμῶν τὰς καρδίας</u> 3.2 εἰς τὸ στηρίξαι ὑμᾶς καὶ παρακαλέσαι
3.1 <u>τὸ λοιπόν</u> <u>προσεύχεσθε, ἀδελφοί, περὶ ἡμῶν</u>	4.1 <u>λοιπόν</u> 5.25 ἀδελφοί, προσεύχεσθε περὶ ἡμῶν
3.3 <u>πιστὸς ὁ κύριος, ὅς</u>	5.24 <u>πιστὸς ὁ καλῶν, ὅς</u>
3.4 <u>ἃ παραγγέλλομεν</u>	4.2 <u>παραγγελίας ἐδώκαμεν.</u>
3.5 (ὁ κύριος) <u>κατευθύναι τὰς καρδίας</u>	3.11 <u>κατευθύναι</u> 3.13 <u>τὰς καρδίας</u>
3.6-7 <u>παραγγέλλομεν ὑμῖν—ἐν</u> (ὀνόματι) <u>τοῦ κυρίου Ἰησοῦ Χριστοῦ—ἀτάκτως περιπατοῦντος—κατ</u>ὰ <u>τὴν παράδοσιν, ἣν παρελάβοσαν παρ' ἡμῶν—αὐτοὶ γὰρ οἴδατε—πῶς δεῖ—</u>ἠτακτήσαμεν	4.1-2 <u>ἐρωτῶμεν καὶ παρακαλοῦμεν ἐν κυρίῳ Ἰησοῦ</u> (which corresponds in detail more with 3.12 than 3.6)—<u>καθὼς παρελάβετε παρ' ἡμῶν—πῶς δεῖ περιπατεῖν—</u>οἴδατε γὰρ 5.14 τοὺς ἀτάκτους 2.1 αὐτοὶ γὰρ οἴδατε (?)
3.8 ἐν κόπῳ καὶ μόχθῳ νυκτὸς καὶ ἡμέρας ἐργαζόμενοι πρὸς τὸ μὴ ἐπιβαρῆσαί τινα ὑμῶν	2.9 κόπον—καὶ τὸν μόχθον· νυκτὸς καὶ ἡμέρας ἐργαζόμενοι πρὸς τὸ μὴ ἐπιβαρῆσαί τινα ὑμῶν
3.9 τύπον—τὸ μιμεῖσθαι ἡμᾶς	1.6-7 μιμηταὶ ἡμῶν—τύπον
3.10 καὶ γὰρ ὅτε ἤμεν πρὸς ὑμᾶς	3.4 καὶ γὰρ ὅτε πρὸς ὑμᾶς ἤμεν

The Literary Relationship of the Two Letters to the Thessalonians

3.10–12 <u>παρηγγέλλομεν ὑμῖν</u>—ἐργάζεσθαι—περιπατο<u>ῦντας ἀτάκτως</u>—<u>ἐργαζομένους</u>—παραγγέλλομεν καὶ <u>παρακαλοῦμεν ἐν κυρίῳ Ἰησοῦ Χριστῷ</u>—μετ<u>ὰ ἡσυχίας ἐργαζόμενοι</u>—<u>ἑαυτῶν</u> (?) [ἄρτον]	4.10–12 <u>παρακαλοῦμεν</u>—<u>ἡσυχάζειν</u>—τ<u>ὰ ἴδια</u> (?)—<u>ἐργάζεσθαι</u>—<u>ὑμῖν παρηγγείλαμεν</u>—περιπατῆ<u>τε</u> 5.14 τοὺς ἀτάκτους 4.1 <u>ἐρωτῶμεν καὶ παρακαλοῦμεν ἐν κυρίῳ Ἰησοῦ</u>
3.15 (<u>μὴ ὡς ἐχθρὸν</u>) <u>ἡγεῖσθε</u>—νουθετεῖτε (i.e., the <u>ἄτακτοι</u>)	5.13–14 <u>ἡγεῖσθαι (ἐν ἀγάπῃ)</u>—<u>νουθετεῖτε τοὺς ἀτάκτους</u>
3.16 <u>αὐτὸς δὲ ὁ κύριος τῆς εἰρήνης</u>	5.23 <u>αὐτὸς δὲ ὁ θεὸς τῆς εἰρήνης</u>
3.18 <u>ἡ χάρις</u> κτλ.	5.28 <u>ἡ χάρις</u> κτλ.

In the first part of this overview the matching words of the succession are already obvious, but nonetheless do not mean very much. The parallelism is markedly interrupted here especially with sections 2 Thess 1:5–12 and 2 Thess 2:1–12, and the relatedness at the beginning is naturally partially documented by the style of the letter. So much more the second part from 2 Thess 2:13 on, in which the majority of the parallel contacts occur, stands out as very important. The structure of the letters here reveals an entirely remarkable uniformity. Should such be possible, unless the latter was dependent upon the earlier letter?

7) *Two parallels are especially highlighted and emphasized because of the surprising exactness of the correspondence.*

First of all both of the greetings are to be considered.[29] No other heading and greeting of Paul's letters is so very closely similar to that greeting of the Second Letter to Thessalonians as that of the first letter, which has been reproduced and is to be found completely even to the very last letter. Thereby the following is especially to be observed and considered:

a) that only here an addition such as ἀπόστολος or δοῦλοι Χριστοῦ is entirely missing after the name of the Apostle and his helpers.

b) that only here the *nomen gentilicium* (Θεσσαλονικέων) is used rather than the circumscription with the place-name.

c) that only here a ἐν θεῷ πατρὶ is found and to be sure exactly at the same position. It is very unusual that for 2 Thess 1:2, despite the ἐν θεῷ πατρὶ κτλ at the closing, the addition ἀπὸ θεοῦ πατρὸς ἡμῶν κτλ still follows it.

Nevertheless the second parallel is more important. It concerns the following passages:

29. See 5 above.

2 Thess 3:8: . . . ἐν κόπῳ καὶ μόχθῳ νυκτὸς καὶ ἡμέρας ἐργαζόμενοι πρὸς τὸ μὴ ἐπιβαρῆσαί τινα ὑμῶν . . . and

1 Thess 2:9: μνημονεύετε γάρ, ἀδελφοί, τὸν κόπον ἡμῶν καὶ τὸν μόχθον· νυκτὸς καὶ ἡμέρας ἐργαζόμενοι πρὸς τὸ μὴ ἐπιβαρῆσαί τινα ὑμῶν . . .

Each time we have here κόπος καὶ μόχθος, each time νυκτὸς καὶ ἡμέρας ἐργάζεσθαι, and each time above all from νυκτός on completely identical word-forms and expressions and not, for example, once ἐργάζεσθαι instead of ἐργαζόμενοι, εἰς τὸ instead of πρὸς τὸ, ὑμᾶς instead of τινα ὑμῶν. The related words of the same meaning which one has compared to those taken from the letters to the Corinthians sound much more divergent and different, for example 2 Cor 11:9: καὶ παρὼν πρὸς ὑμᾶς καὶ ὑστερηθεὶς οὐ κατενάρκησα οὐθενός . . . καὶ ἐν παντὶ ἀβαρῆ ἐμαυτὸν ὑμῖν ἐτήρησα καὶ τηρήσω· (cf. verses 7–8; 1 Cor 4:12; 9:12). Nowhere in any of Paul's authentic letters (except for example the phrases and keywords as found in 1 Cor 5:6; Gal 5:9) can such literal and exact agreement and correspondence at all be documented between two texts of Paul's, even such similar passages and texts as Gal 3:28; 5:14; Col 3:11; Rom 13:9.

With this it seems to me that all important points and parallels have been dealt with. How do we come to terms with and assess this material with these comparisons?

Jülicher[30] has said—and others have similarly interpreted and judged—"so many points of contact and similar content with I Thess are to be explained on the basis of the same situation that underlies them; in the meantime Paul has learned (or he has received no new written reports) almost nothing new or different about the Thessalonians." One will take this thought and proposal into consideration, but it is immediately clear on the basis of the analysis above that such a suggestion provides very little explanation.

When with the opening heading and greeting Silvanus and Timothy are named along with Paul, when with the first portion of the letter the words θλῖψις and ὑπομονή are mentioned, when 2 Thess 2:1 reminds us that Christians are assembling to meet their Lord Jesus Christ with his Parousia, when 2 Thess 3 exhorts the Christians to work with quietness (ἐργάζεσθαι, ἡσυχία, and the ἄτακτοι speaks about ἀτακτεῖν and νουθετεῖν), so perhaps all of this is to be explained on the basis of the continuation of the earlier situation and questions. But the greatest number of parallels here and their characteristics have absolutely nothing to do with a specific

---

30. Jülicher, *Einleitung*, 40, 47. Cf. furthermore p. 27 below.

historical situation. The entire section 2 Thess 2:13—3:5 which mirrors so much of the same content of the first letter could according to its thought and content be found in almost any one of Paul's letters. Also in those passages in which one can rightly point to the similarity of the situations, as for example 2 Thess 3:6–15, the corresponding similarity goes far beyond and exceeds any description of the situation. Such an explanation does not at all suffice to render an understanding of parallelism in the structure of the letter and in the placement and consequential significance of the abundant parallels.

One can and should consider two other matters here. If the second letter comes from Paul's hand, it could at all events have been written only some—at least three months—after the first letter was written. Thus the Apostle could well have been able to remember his earlier composition. He could have unintentionally fallen back—lapsed—into one or another phrase and expression he used for the first letter. Or he could have purposely called to mind what he had written earlier to the community about their eschatological question.[31] Thus we could consider it possible that at that time he possessed and retained some stylistic usage and expressions which then fell from his pen. For example he wrote in the heading ἐν θεῷ πατρὶ rather than ἀπὸ θεοῦ πατρός, or with the joyful greetings and wishes he began with αὐτὸς δὲ ὁ θεός. But on the basis of this consideration and hypothesis only a very few of the similarities can be explained. They change nothing whatsoever about the fact that if Paul were the author of the second letter, then for most all of the related passages and the remarkable pages of exact relationships and wording it could only have been a matter of pure coincidence which brought this about.

It must be coincidence that phrases and exact words precisely occur and correspond with one another when with regard to the nature of the questions no explanation is given for this. It must be coincidence that in the headings of the two letters the exact wording of the first letter is repeated again in the second and is not just similar. It must be coincidence that with 2 Thess 3:8 Paul writes a dozen words almost painfully the same in the same form and order as in 1 Thess 2:9. It must be coincidence that he does not at all touch on the new happenings of the community life of the Thessalonians, and that with the exception of 2 Thess 2:1–12 he does not offer the community any new thoughts or reports from his point of view. It

---

31. Jülicher, *Einleitung*, 3rd and 4th ed. He applies this retrospection concerning the eschatological question to his view of the similar situation. See p. 26 above.

must be coincidence that he lapses unintentionally once more into a very similar series of thoughts as he did months ago. It must be coincidence that his reminiscences occur—heap up—in the same segments which then correspond to those of his earlier letter. It must be coincidence that one must document this characteristic in almost all parts of the second letter. It must be coincidence that the appearance arises that the writer follows with only a few exceptions the exact order and structure of the first letter. It must be coincidence that the above mentioned similarities and parallels occur remarkably in the same order and at the same places of the first letter. It must be coincidence that here and elsewhere verbiage, figures of speech, additions, and sentence forms are to be found which one might consider characteristic of Paul's usage in other letters but which one definitely cannot find.[32] At last for all intents and purposes the real and actual coincidence is that all of these coincidences could concur with one another.

There is no such coincidence. (Such a coincidence simply does not exist.) Therefore the assumption which presupposes it must be false. This is the decisive and crucial fact which to me appears to provide indirectly yet the strongest and most compelling argument.

For it also does not help to attempt to explain this by searching for a special psychological explanation. Bornemann who has sensed the difficulty of the relatedness of the relationship of these two letters more strongly and acutely than most of the advocates of the Pauline origin of them and who actually finds "irrefutable" the conclusion "that the author of the second letter knew and was familiar with the first letter and in some manner was dependent upon it,"[33] has found in just such a psychological reflection the "very simple" resolution to the problem.[34]

He speculates that during the weeks after his sudden departure from Thessalonica Paul might find himself in an ever increasing situation of uncertainty and tension with regard to the new community. At that time he deliberated over everything again and again about that which he recorded in the first letter when with the news that Timothy brought on his return, the tension was dissipated and gave way to a joyful certainty although for

---

32. Here one should take note of the following expressions which have been previously explicated: τοῖς μὴ εἰδόσιν θεὸν 2Thess 1:8; ἔργον πίστεως 2 Thess 1:11; ἐρωτῶμεν δὲ ὑμᾶς, ἀδελφοί 2 Thess 2:1; ἀδελφοὶ ἠγαπημένοι ὑπὸ κυρίου 2 Thess 2:13; περιποίησις 2 Thess 2:14; αὐτὸς δὲ ὁ κύριος 2 Thess 2:16; 3:16; προσεύχεσθε, ἀδελφοί, περὶ ἡμῶν 2 Thess 3:1; κατευθύνειν 2 Thess 3:5, namely in the optative; ἀτάκτως 2 Thess 3:6, 11.

33. Bornemann, *Die Thessalonicherbriefe*, 474, cf. 477.

34. Ibid., 484–85.

the most part this no longer even had any direct meaning for Paul. The first letter then reflects the fruits of that new and inner contemplation and understanding of those weeks. It often easily happens that when we deal at first in-depth and thoroughly with people or other matters, we create thought-associations, twists of thought, and judgments which then emerge in a similar manner once more in the present circumstance. This is often a frequent experience with regard to letters for the same, definite circumstance or occasion, or sermons that deal with the same text. Thus the relatedness of the two letters would be in this manner thoroughly understandable.

But at all events these suppositions are not actual facts, rather only at best possibilities. Let us assume that generally with regard to the inner and contemplative preparation for the first letter this did take place, and furthermore that the earlier thoughts of the Apostle Paul established themselves in just such a manner: what would be then explained by this? Perhaps particular matters. For example, the expression, ἐπισυναγωγῆς ἐπ᾽ αὐτόν, 2 Thess 2:1, would well be once more understood from such that from Paul's point of view his earlier comments and statements concerning the hope for the future had a rather exact meaning. But should we also believe that he concerned himself with such colorless and dreary wishes and admonitions found in 1 Thess 3:11—4:2 and likewise already formed them in his intellect before the composition and thereafter carried them in his memory for a long time? Precisely that material from the first letter which one would like first of all to believe[35] preoccupied the thoughts of Paul for quite some time, the personal conflicts and disputes found in 1 Thessalonians 2–3 and the eschatological instructions and teaching in 1 Thessalonians 4–5, do *not* reoccur completely in the second letter. But generally though Bornemann has most carefully and diligently drawn attention to the parallels, he has not sufficiently realized that it is not simply the total of contacts which must be comprehended, rather much more exactly the special congruence of the specifics as well as also the smallest and extrinsic aspects of the parallels, and beyond that the actual positions and placings of the parallels. More often than not, no such good appeal to the memory and subconscious recollection exists over and against these matters.

One must recognize that the matter does not concern the alternative whether or not the author of this writing was "familiar" with the first letter or was "somehow dependent upon it." The question must be much more

---

35. Ibid. Cf. contradictory comments Bornemann makes on 484 and for example on 266.

The Authenticity of the Second Letter to the Thessalonians

specifically and definitely grasped, and this is very important. It must read as follows: *Did the author have this letter in front of him and did he himself look into the actual letter during the writing of the second letter?* If one is actually permitted to conclude anything at all from what was said concerning the position and sequence of the parallels, about the repetition of actual words, and in another regard the surprising exactness of single points of contact, so one must also conclude the following: *We have here the characteristic mark of literary plagiarism.* Only this assumption explains all aspects of the relatedness. Every other assumption explains only an indefinite relationship from a general perspective, that which is actually conspicuous. For then the relatedness must relegate all of the special parallels and similarities once more to pure coincidence. For such a fading memory of earlier matters which were either written or read earlier does not call forth similarities and aspects which are discussed above from numbers 4–7.

Despite all this if Paul himself should have written this letter, then there remains only the assumption that with the conception and composition of it he had his own earlier letter in front of him. But is that not really a serious, reasonable, and debatable possibility?[36]

With his hypothesis Zahn places us in the situation—it is certainly the only conceivable one here—that allows us to approach this possibility more closely. He holds it to be

> impossible that Paul's letters, just so as the writer of them put them on paper during the dictation, were then immediately sent to the communities.... As a rule there was the requirement for a subsequent revision of the completed, dictated letter along with (!) the completion of a final copy. During the time when this copy was sent to the place of its destination, the first draft of the letter would have remained for a long time in the hands of the Apostle and the writer. For Paul who was extremely busy and whose conscious temperament was extremely excitable, just here in this case he had the convenient opportunity to read through the rough draft of 1 Thess, if and should it have been available, once more before he dictated 2 Thess.[37]

Zahn has not exactly thoroughly instructed and informed his readers about the extant relatedness between the two letters. Yet this hypothesis—the

36. Cf. Bornemann, *Die Thessalonicherbriefe*, 492; Jülicher, *Einleitung*, 39; Zahn, *Einleitung*, 172. The hypothesis that the second letter precedes the first letter which would then yield another factual situation may be left to its own for the present.

37. Zahn, *Einleitung*, 178.

final copy (*Reinschrift*) seems to be gradually summoned and relied upon with a greater role for New Testament questions—betrays a stronger appreciation for the difficulty at hand, even though it has cropped up and arisen as the back door. The conjecture therefore arises to the contrary that it might have not been so entirely natural "that during the dictation, the structure (!) and words (!) of the earlier letter remained in Paul's consciousness," as Zahn shortly beforehand assures us.[38] I do not know to what extent this assumption, of which he otherwise, so far as I see, makes no use of whatsoever, accounts for the source of these facts and matters other than the unpleasant similarity of the two letters. I also do not want to determine at all whether or not this assumption is possible, and how on the basis of it the darkness and unpolished parlance of many of Paul's words and expressions might be explained, made up, and formulated.[39] But I fear that when we seek to save this letter with this helpful final copy (*Reinschrift*), we will corrupt the Apostle.

Certainly one should not place any unjustified demands and pretenses on Paul. His letters do not have to be always meaningful, important, and brilliant. Why with a composition should he have not even relied on the structure and thoughts of a letter which he had just directed to another addressee? He would have done nothing more than what many other letter-writers have done both before and after him. Yet it is difficult for the reader to imagine a reclusive Paul who has just read his earlier letter and then allows himself to become dependent upon it for the same community, who is so wanting for words that in more than half of the letter he can hardly fathom how to strike up a new tone, and who again and again uses the same words and expressions at the exact same place in the text. Such a prospect and description does not become more plausible by means of the circumstance itself that he was "very busy," and of an "extremely excitable temperament," and can be taken seriously from his word from Phil 3:1, "to write you always the same, does not bother me." However one approaches the matter, one cannot get around the following dilemma: if the matters deal only with Paul's unconscious and already faded memory, so then the most extraordinary and most important similarities of all those actual,

---

38. Ibid., 175.

39. Laurent, Untitled Entry, *Neutestamentliche Studien*, 4–5. The question whether or not Paul allowed his letters to be copied has already been considered by Laurent. He has rejected this for several reasons. Paul did not have the means to buy paper for a second copy; he along with his helpers did not have the time for it; and he did not value his letters enough to make the effort to preserve the original text.

extant similarities of the two letters remain to be explained. If, however, one postulates for Paul such a fresh and exact knowledge of the first letter, as it is necessary to do in order to make these similarities at all understandable, so an entire half of the letter must be attributed to Paul's own plagiarism. A way out can first be found when one has explained how, for Paul's memory precisely in the moment at the same time as he wrote, both aspects could have been the same: known and unknown, clear and faded.

Until now our discussion has been concerned only with the relatedness of the two letters. But one must also consider the differences. At least one observation can be made here, one that is important enough to be added and attached immediately. When one compares the contents of the two documents, it becomes especially evident that section 1 Thess 2:1—3:10 has absolutely no counterpart in the entirely of our letter, i.e., the historical, personal discussions and comments have been omitted. It can be surmised here that there was no current reason once more for a repetition of that review of the Apostle's first mission in Thessalonica as is found in 1 Thess 2:1–12 because the first letter had already presented that. Likewise it cannot be expected that Paul would have spoken once more about the return of Timothy and its impact on him 1 Thess 3:1–10. Yet one misses the contact and mention of another point that dominates the entire presentation of 1 Thess 2:17—3:13. Most emphatically and, so it seems, very intentionally Paul speaks here of his yearning, his intention, and the prospect to visit and call on the community once more. But the second letter does not mention one word about this. This has long been noticed and has attracted our attention.[40] An explanation has also, of course, been offered.[41] Perhaps as Paul wrote this second letter, the work of his mission in Corinth has simply pushed his earlier thoughts about a visit and second meeting into the background. I do not dispute this possibility, but I do contest that this possibility suffices as a thorough explanation. For it is not unusual or strange that the Apostle might, on the basis of new circumstances, alter his earlier plan and his previous hope. But here the matter is simply that the very expression of a thought or plan is missing. Not only is there no mention of the visit with which he had personally just concerned himself, but he writes nothing of his wish for such a journey with which he had occupied himself very intensively with regard to the community. Expressed another way, he simply

---

40. Holtzmann, "Zum zweiten Thessalonicherbreif," 105–6. Once more he has accentuated it here.

41. Bornemann, *Die Thessalonicherbriefe*, 483. Cf. 475.

omits here that which very much affects the interest of the community just as his own. Furthermore, should he have had that very letter in which he had discussed that question so precisely in his memory such that either against his will or by his own choice, it remained in other regards entirely excluded from the sphere of his thoughts!

However, if an unknown author wrote under the name of Paul, then the matter is simple enough. As he relied on the first letter, so he could have at least actually begun with the historical and personal section. Yet for him these matters were the least important in that document, for they did not contain anything at all instructive or universally true. Naturally he did not by any means understand the appeal which precisely the personal aspects of Paul's letter offer us today. Thus Paul's thoughts and aspirations for another visit disappeared along with the rest.

This point also thus supports the result and conclusion to which our entire study and research presses on: *that it was not Paul who wrote this letter, rather another.*

Should perhaps this other writer be known to us? Should it have been Timothy of 2 Thess 1:1, named along with the other senders of the letter? With this assumption along also with other characteristics of the letter Spitta[42] has sought to make its relatedness to the first letter clear and understandable[43] such that he knows to recognize and value these aspects just as Bornemann has done. Timothy wrote the second letter under the mandate and name of Paul (and Silvanus) while Paul engaged himself directly in the writing only with the concluding remarks of 2 Thess 3:17–18. Thus the letter is authentic even though it does not come from Paul.

Second Thessalonians 2:5 is especially important for Spitta: Οὐ μνημονεύετε ὅτι ἔτι ὢν πρὸς ὑμᾶς ταῦτα ἔλεγον ὑμῖν. The first person singular occurs here rather than the usual ἡμεῖς. Timothy is referring to himself with the ἔτι ὢν πρὸς ὑμᾶς as he remembers his last visit in Thessalonica about which the first letter speaks.

Yet his hypothesis would by no means explain the actual aspects and relationships of the letter as long as one remains at least with Spitta with only Timothy's lively memory of the earlier writing of the first letter. But it is uncalled for here to explicate this, since this hypothesis has already been proven to be impossible. It is my opinion, for example, that the arguments

---

42. Spitta, *Zur Geschichte*, 109ff.
43. Ibid., 126.

provided by Bornemann[44] and Zahn[45] are a justifiable refutation. How should the mere first person singular point to Timothy, when in the first letter the "I" of 1 Thess 3:5 and 5:27 is admittedly Paul although Timothy is the author? Also when one suggests[46] that the readers might have known that the ἔτι ὢν πρὸς ὑμᾶς refers to the previous visit of Timothy because according to the hypothesis only he of the other forerunners of the parousia might have spoken to them, there remains only a mere ἔλεγον for Timothy in a letter that bears the name of Paul at beginning with its heading. How should the readers have concluded from the handwriting of Timothy ("in contrast to that of Paul in the closing remarks of 2 Thess 3:17")[47] that the first person singular designates him, when this same handwriting in the first letter, 1 Thess 3:5; 5:27, does not prevent them from thinking about Paul? Above all, however, how did Paul ever come to the point of verifying with the solemn remark of 2 Thess 3:17 this letter as his own, precisely this letter with which he had the least role to play?

The author must have been a later writer, and *the letter is fiction.*

---

44. Bornemann, *Die Thessalonicherbriefe*, 529ff.; 513ff.
45. Zahn, *Einleitung*, 166.
46. Spitta, *Zur Geschichte*, 125.
47. Ibid.

CHAPTER II

OBJECTIONS TO AN EARLY FICTION
The Writer's Purpose and Situation

The most important objection that one can raise against this conclusion has played a remarkably insignificant role in the historical-critical discussion on both sides. I am referring here to the chronological assessment and determination of this second letter.

When in 2 Thess 2:4 the man of lawlessness is alluded to, whereby he will seat himself in the Temple of God full of his sacrilegious exaltation, so the existence of Jerusalem is apparently presupposed and it is thereby evident that the date of composition is obviously before the year AD 70. During this time Kern, with his well-known and important study,[1] also placed this letter and this date that many more recent scholars have advocated, such as Schmiedel.

But one must admit that these scholars did very little to address the difficulty and raise the awareness of it, which plagues and argues against this viewpoint.[2] Thereby I completely reject the possible reference to Nero

---

1. Kern, "Über 2 Thess 2:1–12." 145.
2. Holtzmann, *Lehrbuch*, 216. "Incidentally today it is not a question as to whether or not the letter should be pushed forward into a timeframe after the apostolic period, but if rather it reaches back into the lifetime of the Apostle and accordingly must have actually been written soon after 1 Thess around 54 AD." But his observations sound differently in his later article: Holtzmann, "Zum zweiten Thessalonikerbriefs," 107.

with 2 Thess 2:1–12, for which the timespan of AD 68–70 would be a possibility at all events since the reference to Nero was primarily a simple and concrete conclusion devoid of any mysticism. Nevertheless, it is certainly all but impossible to assume a composition of the letter before the year AD 70 if the passage 2 Thess 2:1–12 actually refers to Nero. But this difficulty itself is actually negated and thus omitted along with the implausible reference to Nero. Opposed to this, another objection remains that is certainly not of lesser importance.

It is actually quite difficult that soon after Paul's death such a strange letter bearing his name should have been circulated. Above all it is a very difficult matter that this letter must have been addressed to a single, definite community, even that of the Thessalonians. For this assumption is hardly to be avoided.

Admittedly the place and destination given with the heading per se does not at all prove that this pseudepigraphical letter was actually addressed and intended for Thessalonica. Even if the writer had nothing whatsoever to do with the actual community in Thessalonica or wanted to have, there could very well have been other reasons that led him to choose this address. This possibility alone is dependent upon assumptions. Assuming that Paul's letter to the Thessalonians was used and copied by someone far from Thessalonica, so that presupposes that this letter as well as certainly others of Paul's letters have found a wide circulation in the church. Is this to be considered likely before the year AD 70? It might be. But that assumption already presupposes a very high regard and esteem in the church for Paul's letters. Without such, it would have made no sense for a Christian in Asia Minor or Rome or somewhere else, who in his or her hometown or in "the" church wished to find a hearing, to conceal a personal name with that of Paul's. Can one assume or concede such an authority for Paul's letters before the year AD 70 only a few years after his death?

With such an early composition of the letter we must have sought, as it seems, for the recipients of the letter either in Thessalonica or in a community that stood in a relationship with that of Thessalonica, and moreover who also believe that someone from this community itself had written and produced this pseudonymous letter. If that were the case, how then should we arrive at a satisfactory resolution? How should such a letter, one that certainly encountered many potent and enthusiastic voices in Thessalonica—for that would have to be concluded from 2 Thess 2:2—have actually been accepted by many of the community members who had seen the Apostle face to face and had received his first and perhaps others of this letters but knew nothing about this writing? Could the author of such a letter even hope that one would accept it without first receiving an explanation as to why now this letter has come to light?

In other words it must be concluded that a fictional letter can *a priori* only be held as a possibility at a much later date, and namely only in the case that the writer of the second letter did not at all intend that it be written for Thessalonica.³

Totally independent of these reflections still another consideration leads to the same thought and conclusion. If we are actually dealing here with a pseudonymous writing, so then the assertion of 2 Thess 3:17—the concluding remark of Paul himself in "every letter" as a sign of its authenticity—is only to be understood when many of Paul's letters already existed from which such a statement could be prescinded. The expression, ἐν πάσῃ ἐπιστολῇ, presumes already a plurality of known letters. Since only the Letter to the Galatians, the First Letter to the Corinthians, and the Letter to the Colossians explicitly speak of these writings from Paul's⁴ own hand, it is therefore very possible that the author was familiar with all of them.⁵ Or if supposedly it was common in other circles or communities to speak of such a custom associated with Paul, then he simply reproduced this statement on which this familiarity was based. By all means the First Letter to the Thessalonians must also be considered. But when one knew of these four letters,⁶ so presumably one was familiar with even more. Thus, if 2 Thess 3:17 was not written by Paul, it clearly documents an entire collection of Paul's letters that is not at all conceivable before the year AD 70.

---

3. Schmiedel, Untitled Entry, *Handkommentar*, 10–11.

4. Aside from Phm 1:19 that does not belong to this series.

5. Gal 6:11 may well have been composed on the basis of an analogy taken from 1 Cor 16:21; Col 4:18, even if these words should originally refer to the entire letter.

6. Or three, if one will not accept the authenticity of the Letter to the Colossians, which I assume.

The Authenticity of the Second Letter to the Thessalonians

However if a long time after the death of Paul at another location someone wrote a letter for which the place of its destination, Thessalonica, was solely intended as a cover, then the writer did not have to be at all concerned about the reception of that letter in faraway Macedonia. For then the recipients for whom it was intended were just as little interested in Thessalonica as the writer himself. For them, it solely depended on the fact that Paul himself was speaking to them. But with this assumption we certainly have the responsibility to explain how the writer came to the decision to disguise his letter as a letter to the Thessalonians. I am assuming here that this explanation can be provided. Then the passage about the Temple of God that appears to demand an early date for the writing of the letter becomes a difficulty that cannot be concealed.

It would seem to be appropriate to make this postulate known here. Nonetheless it is advisable to present this argument at a later time.

First of all, let us search for an answer to another often mentioned objection. If this letter is fiction, then the entire composition is intended as a riddle. We choose here to deal with this question not simply to explain away the objection. At all events it is essential to make the attempt to conceive of the letter in its historical context under that prerequisite. Thus one will have the opportunity to closely elucidate a point that at first might have meaning among the reasons against the authenticity of the letter with regard to the discussion above.

A letter such as ours cannot simply be an exercise in Pauline rhetorical style, also not a sermon, and not simply an edifying address for an undetermined audience. That is very evident. Whoever is making the effort to appear here as Paul (2 Thess 3:17) is pursuing a definite goal. Otherwise his purpose would be meaningless.

If anything about the letter reveals to us the purpose of the author, then it must be 2 Thess 2:1–12. Here we found the only passage where a definite idea is extensively developed of which the first letter makes no mention whatsoever. Here the word-parallels cease to appear, and at this juncture the *sequence* of the parallels listed above is most noticeably interrupted. Here we encounter at the beginning the one definite element that we are able to perceive and assess with regard to the historical situation of the first letter. It is no mere coincidence that all of this emerges and concurs at this point. Everything here points to a certain direction, and it indicates that the writer himself is speaking and at last says what he really wants to say. The dependence of the other sections of the second letter viewed over against those of the first letter are hereby even more markedly highlighted by means of this contrast.

Besides this section only 2 Thess 3:6–16 could be of any significant importance from a secondary point of view—that passage where the idleness of some has been so severely rebuked. For the moment, however, we will leave that matter for later.

Certainly the writer has not simply intended to present a theoretical message of apocalyptic teaching, or as Kern said,[7] to impart an apocalyptic vision that he has seen. Rather the instruction serves another purpose, either to verify or rebut a purpose. That follows assuredly from the introduction of the passage, 2 Thess 2:2, 3a. The writer encounters a viewpoint that turns one's head (σαλευθῆναι ἀπὸ τοῦ νοός) and terribly freightens (θροεῖσθαι), and that appears to him to be nothing more than deception and deceit depicted with 2 Thess 2:3. One cannot seriously consider the possibility here that he has taken this occasion to make up his own apocalyptic discourse. The definite reference to those things that were significant for the formation of this agitation and uproar (μήτε διὰ πνεύματος μήτε διὰ λόγου μήτε δι' ἐπιστολῆς ὡς δι' ἡμῶν), so also the emphasis on the additional sentence, μή τις ὑμᾶς ἐξαπατήσῃ κατὰ μηδένα τρόπον that contains his warning, readily preclude this possibility. Furthermore one cannot imagine how and for what reason he might have thought up and have written such a fiction. Here the actual events of his time and from his community must have been displaced back into Paul's time, and the writer had accordingly a definite and practical purpose for this.

The very opinion he opposes is referred to with these words: ὡς ὅτι ἐνέστηκεν ἡ ἡμέρα τοῦ κυρίου. Here it is very clear that this cannot mean that the Day of the Lord has already occurred[8] or that all hope for it is futile. If only οὐκ ἐνέστκεν had been written here!

---

7. Kern, "Über 2 Thess 2:1–12," 214.

8. Bahnsen, Untitled Entry, *Jahrbücher*, VI, 681ff. It is Bahnsen's view that the unique Coming of Christ has been denied or misconstrued, and he compares this to 2 Tim 2:18

Not an exhaustion of the expectation of the Parousia, not any doubt about the Lord for whom one has so long futilely waited as to whether or not he will actually come, but rather instead the teaching about the Anti-Christ is meant to appease and comfort. That viewpoint has often arisen before,[9] but it is completely impossible.

However one translates ἐνέστηκεν ἡ ἡμέρα τοῦ κυρίου with either, "The Day of the Lord stands before us," and is about to come, or more precisely, "It is there, it has come," the assertion is being made that one stands immediately on the threshold of events of the Last Day.[10] Contrary to this the writer can have only wanted to say: "No, not yet!" He does not say this with meager words, but according to his instruction concerning the End Time he wants to make the consequences precisely known. "At first" the decline must come and the man of lawlessness must be revealed. But when for the time being this revelation has been "prevented," so then the Day of the Lord cannot be about to happen.

I do not mean that the composition and structure of this chapter can be clearly and completely described according to this point of view. Certainly it can be questioned why the aspect of time has not been more specifically developed. The writer himself has *not* emphasized the fact that the presence of a κατέχον has more than ever extended the Parousia, although the reader must reach this conclusion based on text itself. It is also clearly

on page 702–3.

9. Cf. Baur, *Paulus*, 487. Also without Bahnsen's explanation of ἐνέστηκεν, one would want to lend credibility to 2 Thess 2 as to why the Parousia cannot take place so soon. One has already waited so long without avail. Grimm has surely and rightly so credited Baur with a *quid pro quo*. (Grimm, *Die Echtheit*; Baur, *Studien und Kritiken*, 789–90)

10. Zahn, *Einleitung*, 167–68. Zahn gives his version of this passage. Since the presupposed earlier explanation given to the community of the Thessalonians cannot have been completely forgotten, a preliminary report must be given to them to let them know that the Anti-Christ has already come in the person of Caligula. (An audacious conjecture!) With the end of his life (AD 41) "The Day of the Lord" (according to this opinion) has already been ushered in, i.e., the epoch has begun during which at any minute one had expected the visible Second Coming of Christ or Parousia. But this conceptual expectation is therefore not feasible because Paul would have confronted such a thought very differently. He would have had to say: The Anti-Christ has not yet appeared as one would believe, and he is not the one whom one has pronounced him to be. He says only: the Anti-Christ must come first before the Parousia, i.e., he emphasizes that matter from which the disputed expectation has arisen. But furthermore if the "Day of the Lord" has already existed for more than ten years (ἐνέστηκεν)—in and of itself a most strange conception—, so it is not very easy to understand how now the agitation and tumult could suddenly arise of which 2 Thess 2:2 speaks.

evident that the reason for the explanation here does not resonate once more in the second part from 2 Thess 2:8–12, and that the length and depth of the description which particularly concerns the appearance and impact of the ἄνομος seems to be somewhat diminished in this regard. However as one reflects on this, there is nonetheless no doubt about the fact that it is the foremost aim and goal of this description to correct the view of the believers concerning the immediate coming of the End Time.

It has very often been said that another eschatological expectation can be detected here rather than that described by the First Letter to the Thessalonians; and at the same time one has asserted that our letter develops this teaching intentionally with an oppositional relationship to the first letter. In this regard not only would the 1 Thess 4:15 be considered, according to which Paul includes himself among the ones who will live to see the Parousia (cf. 1 Thess 4:17), but much more rather the statement of 1 Thess 5:1–4 that the Day of the Lord is to come like a thief in the night. Thus the destruction will suddenly come when one speaks of peace and security, an expressed expectation that with 1 Thess 5:1 is placed virtually under the rubric of χρόνοι καὶ καιροί of the Parousia.

It is without question that two letters are different regarding this matter. But it is rather doubtful that such a contradiction would arise from a comparison to the questionable passages that would therefore preclude the actual identity of the writer.[11]

By all means there is nothing in the second letter that states that the Parousia will not come for a very long time. If the "Secret of Iniquity" is already at work (ἤδη ἐνεργεῖται 2 Thess 2:7), the Parousia does not appear here also to be delayed for a long time. On the other hand, the first letter does not at all record the words, ἐνέστηκεν ἡ ἡμέρα τοῦ κυρίου, and thus allows for a time before the arrival of the events of the Parousia.

Nonetheless, the difference of the two letters does not appear to be clearly enough grasped with these remarks. Is it then also consistent and accordable that with 1 Thess 5:1–11 the coming of the Parousia is viewed virtually as unpredictable while according to 2 Thess 2:1–12 the nearness of the Parousia can be known and recognized with actual events?[12] Here

---

11. Cf. Holtzmann, *Einleitung*, 215; Holtzmann, *Lehrbuch*, II 190ff.; Schmiedel, Untitled Entry, *Handkommentar*, II, 1, 8–9 on the one hand. But for the opposing view on the other hand cf. Spitta, *Zur Geschichte*, I, 109ff.; Bornemann, *Die Thessalonicherbriefe*, 534ff.; Jülicher, *Einleitung*, 42ff.; Zahn, *Einleitung*, 181.

12. It is interesting that a related argument is to be found earlier with the view of Caius that was contested by Hippolytus. Caius disputes the miracle of Rev 8:8, 12, whereby

one can readily refer to the apocalyptic chapters of the Gospels (cf. also the Apocalypse), whereby the sayings of the sudden, unpredictable Coming of Christ are placed directly next to discourses about the signs of the Coming of the Parousia.[13] Perhaps, however, this reference is not quite appropriate, since one should first of all determine whether or not one is dealing here with opposing expectations of a different origin.[14] But then is the concept that the Day of the Lord is unpredictable negated and overturned by 2 Thess 2:1–12? That can hardly be asserted if the signs themselves are also unpredictable. If one should want to calculate how much time must pass before the spectacle of the ἄνομος takes place[15] with his veneration in the entire world and his journey to Jerusalem in order to verify that Christ could not at all come like a thief in the night, so that is all just a bit too rational and more the chronology of reason rather than apocalyptic fantasy. For such fantasy "reasons" a totally different way and much faster than human reason. Or one could say that it does not reason at all; only the intellect reasons. To be sure Jewish scholars of the time of Justin[16] calculated the "3 ½ times" of the Anti-Christ according to Daniel to be 350 years. But that is first of all only an erudite, scholarly matter that hardly comes into question here. Certainly, though, one matter cannot be denied. At the time that Paul wrote 1 Thess 5:1–11, he did not think about and consider the spread and divulgence of the Parousia. But the question as far as I am concerned is only if actually a certain change and self-contradiction is not thoroughly comprehensible. The provocation that called forth the explanation of 2 Thess 2:1–12 was not to be found anyway in the first letter; but just now it was necessary to suppress and quiet the impatience and tumult.

Yet certainly with regard to 2 Thess 2:5, Paul must have taught similarly in Thessalonica even without this provocation and at a time before the first letter as it is reported with the section of 2 Thess 2:1–12. It appears on its own that this is to be understood here. Eschatological expectation can be easily expanded upon. The same Christ could himself view the prerequisite

he cites and relies on 1 Thess 5:2–3. Cf. the *Capita Hippolyti Adversus Caius*, 241–42. Hippolytus counters Caius among other points with a likewise contemporary argument: "This assertion that the Day of the Lord is to come 'like a thief' is a reference to those unbelievers who themselves are the darkness. For the true believers are children of the light, who do not walk in the darkness," 241.

13. Cf. Spitta, *Zur Geschichte*, I, 129–30; Bornemann, *Die Thessalonicherbriefe*, 536.
14. Holtzmann, "Zum zweiten Thessalonicherbrief," 97–98. His view is similar.
15. Schmiedel, Untitled Entry, *Handkommentar*, 8–11.
16. Justin Martyr, *Dialogue with Trypho*, 32.

events and signs associated with the catastrophe together as one, and yet at the same time look beyond them to the primary matter. But on the other hand he could again emphasize at another time that certain events must precede the event. Yet generally speaking, is it very probable that the teaching about the preparation for the Last Day (i.e., this chapter that presents Jewish eschatology) was perhaps thoroughly foreign and extraneous to Paul himself as he wrote the first letter? Here I do not include the expectation of the Anti-Christ. That is a question that one is not permitted to ignore. With 1 Cor 7:26 he speaks of ἐνεστῶσα ἀνάγκη. That, to be sure, is not the Parousia itself, but on the basis of it one could at all events realize that the Day of the Lord is coming. Is this short reference to a definite group of eschatological conceptions and images also incompatible with 1 Thess 5:1–4? Or should Paul have first adopted the expectation and conception of this ἀνάγκη subsequently? Who would want to believe this?

A reasoning of this kind is perhaps not convincing for everyone, but it is difficult to refute. Certainly one is permitted and actually must take note of the fact that in two so very different letters, one that follows so quickly after the other, it is clearly evident that Paul speaks so very differently about these matters. It is particularly striking that with the one passage where he explicitly deals with the question of the χρόνοι and καιροί, where he remarks that the readers would know for certain about the sudden coming of the Parousia, he does not at all think about the things that according to 2 Thess 2:5 he would have wanted to teach in Thessalonica.[17] When this alone is actually sufficient to raise serious suspicion against our letter, it is not sufficient by itself to boost the suspicion beyond a level of mere distrust without the reception of other reasons.

It is another matter when the doubt about the authenticity of the letter arises from other considerations as well as actually from those reasons that we have developed above. Then the conspicuous immediately becomes a definite hint and pointer. With a letter that follows so closely upon the first letter to the Thessalonians, it cannot be coincidental that when precisely the primary chapter is related to the content of a distinctive passage of the original draft, it proceeds in a completely different direction. There must be a relationship. Therefore the writer himself specifies for good measure clearly enough with the words ὑπὲρ τῆς παρουσίας τοῦ κυρίου . . . καὶ ἡμῶν ἐπισυναγωγῆς ἐπ' αὐτόν that he is referring back to 1 Thess 4:13–18.

---

17. Cf. Hilgenfeld, *Einleitung*, 648; Untitled Entry, *Zeitschrift*, 250.

Moreover this reference itself becomes certainly evident since in chapter 2 of the second letter nothing special is mentioned about the ἐπισυναγωγή.[18]

The writer, in this case, only wants to ward off the expectation of the immediate proximity of the Parousia where it is presented in the first letter as it seems to be especially mentioned with 1 Thess 5:1–4, and replace it with an entirely other view that further delays and postpones it. It is not clear at this juncture if he understood 1 Thess 5:1–4 this way or if there were others who did. *Either* he had the intention to oppose Paul on this matter because he disapproved of it and held it to be dangerous; *or* he had the firm belief that Paul meant the same thing as he, and he wants to give a definite direction to the matter with his own words to avoid a false meaning.

Was it possible to find this opinion in the first letter? That letter does not actually state that the Day of the Lord is here or is immediately afoot. It does not even say that it is near[19] but only that the Parousia will suddenly descend upon those who are confident, arrogant, and careless. However, there is no doubt that one could relate this pronouncement to the immediate coming of the Parousia.[20] To be sure it is certain that this expectation could not have originated from the letter itself. As for that matter *no document from the past could assert the view that the moment of the Parousia was about to occur at that time* unless that text or document had contained apocalyptic longings and characteristics. On the other hand, the expectation that the Day of the Lord is imminent could have arisen another way by means of prophecies or through definite events. If that were the case, then the practical exegesis of that day could well have enlivened the words of Paul without scruple. One could say that the Apostle himself verified this very expectation with his sayings.[21] Even that what he has said is fulfilling itself now, for the Day of the Lord is really coming like a thief in the night: no one should count on a long delay.[22] One could perhaps refer to

---

18. Schmiedel is correct with his comment about 2 Thess 2:1.

19. Zahn, *Einleitung*, 167.

20. The expectation that the Parousia could suddenly come has naturally been expressed elsewhere in order to placate and assuage the doubt that arose about the Coming of the Lord. Thus the image of the thief in the night can be found in 2 Pet 3:10. Cf. the word ἐξαίφνης in 1 Clem 23:5.

21. Cf. Jülicher (3,4), *Einleitung*, 48.

22. Just how close the "soon" and the "suddenly" are tangent to one another is clearly shown by *1 Clem* 23:5: ἐπ' ἀληθείας· ταχὺ καὶ ἐξαίφνης τελειωθήσεται τὸ βούλημα αὐτοῦ κτλ.

Objections to an Early Fiction

the general comfort and security mentioned in 1 Thess 5:3 as a sign of the last hour.[23]

Furthermore this appraisal reaches its complete conclusion with the acclaim of these words: δι' ἐπιστολῆς ὡς δι' ἡμῶν from 2 Thess 2:2. It can be shown that in some sense one is reminiscing here about the content of the first letter; so on its own it becomes clear that with that letter the immediate proximity of the Parousia was alluded to and confirmed. But it may be asserted that totally aside from these words everything points to the conclusion that with the eschatological instruction of 2 Thess 2:1–12 a deliberate relationship to the first letter can be assumed.

The writer is addressing those who hold the view that the Coming of Christ is nearer than he assumes. What more do we learn about them?

Here with 2 Thess 2:2 we find the two expressions: σαλευθῆναι ἀπὸ τοῦ νοὸς and θροεῖσθαι. Certainly the first one refers definitely enough to the present uproar. Yet it means more than that since the writer *judges* the sentiments and mood of those for whom he writes, he misses sobriety and discretion. The second expression appears to be more important. The word, θροεῖσθαι, certainly does not need to mean anything more than excitement that has arisen from sudden surprise, generally a disturbance of temperament that robs one of one's composure.[24] Nonetheless, I believe that one is permitted to translate the word with the expression "to become frightened."[25] The parallels of Mark 13:7 and Matt 24:6 suggest this. If the meaning of the word should be broader, the writer is surely not thinking generally about upheaval, for the commotion must have had a definite

---

23. Holtzmann, "Zum zweiten Thessalonicherbrief," 100. Here he places not only 1 Thess 5:1–4 but also 1 Thess 4:15,17 in the foreground (cf. 43 above). The discrepancy of Paul's expectation that he and most of his followers would live to see the Parousia soon over and against the ever ongoing experience to the contrary has at long last called for a correction. This motif is actually the first and most resounding reason that brought about the replacement of the first letter with a new and redacted version. I am not at all convinced by this argument. For I am not able to conceive of the idea as to how one with these words should have justified and constituted the expectation of the immediate coming of the Day of the Lord that would have only been possible during Paul's lifetime. Yet to be sure it is precisely this view against which the writer turns with his opposition. It would be another matter if he wanted to counteract the danger of the lapsing of the hope of the Parousia. One would not have to abandon the assumption that the expression of 2 Thess 2:1 (especially ἐπισυναγωγή) refers back to 1 Thess 4:14, 17, because 1 Thess 5:1 then actually appears to be the primary emphasis. Our division of the chapters does not bother the writer.

24. See von Hofmann.

25. Bahnsen, Untitled Entry, *Jahrbücher*, 702, I thoroughly reject his conclusions.

strain or character. Moreover he is hardly thinking simply about bewilderment, such as that of joy that can bring fulfillment of a superior yearning, but rather he is concerned with consternation and fright.

Alongside the emphasis of the glowing and enthusiastic hope of early Christianity, the element of the horrific and terrible aspects of the picture and concept of the Last Judgment has been, for the most part, strongly underestimated.[26] If the threat of the Last Judgment plays such a role in primitive Christianity, then that is clearly a cue. One is not saying that a Christian community did not need to fear final judgment. Nonetheless it is thoroughly natural that the thought of it, namely as soon as the fateful hour itself appeared to strike, produced above all great fear and terrifying feelings. The same message that caused such people to tremble could certainly bring others to celebration and enthusiastic elation. But the majority of Christians cannot be placed on the level of enthusiastic martyrs and leading visionaries. Namely with regard to the less independent, less mature, average Christians, it was much more natural to assume fear rather than joy; and above all the "Dies Irae" always exercised its power.[27] With our passage, moreover, the expression, ἡ ἡμέρα τοῦ κυρίου, already called forth at first the concept of the Day of Wrath and the End of the World rather than the Day of Salvation. It is thus certain that when the first letter speaks of αἰφνίδιος ὄλεθρος precisely with the saying of 1 Thess 5:3, to which 2 Thess 2:1–12 will especially retrospectively refer, it does not at all detract from the view that here only the people of darkness are threatened with their doom. From the content of 2 Thess 2:3–12 there is nothing more that can be surmised, for it is clear that there is no mention of the tranquility of wishful longing.

As for a further specific support for our view it is clear that in the time of antiquity the church explained the word, θροεῖσθαι, with direct reference to the horrific fright of the Last Judgment. This is proved with Hippolytus's commentary on the Book of Daniel. It may be irrelevant that the Slavic text for 2 Thess 2:2, Book IV, chapter 21 states: "so that you will not *mourn*."[28]

---

26. Wernle, *Die Anfänge*, 373–74. Belatedly I see that Wernle has stated the matter similarly if not exactly the same way.

27. Schmiedel z. St.; Schmiedel, Untitled Entry, *Handkommentar*. Against this view Schmiedel has stated the following: "The writer did not for example fear the great fright, because really the joy was nearer."

28. See the edition of Bonwetsch and Achelis I 1, 237. Bonwetsch considers the possibility that a θρηνῆτε occurred in the original text (236). In the Greek text he reads θορυβῆσθε correctly.

But nevertheless Book IV, chapter 21 clearly shows that Hippolytus himself and others along with him understood θροεῖσθαι as we do. However, it is advantageous to present the entire context in which this passage is to be found. Hippolytus tells a story of two episodes in chapters 18 and 19 of Book IV with the purpose of opposing a premature expectation of the End Time, of which not without interest at least the second in chapter 19 is consistent with our text.[29]

A bishop of Pontus who was pious and humble began to prophesy to his brothers just like a prophet, not with the written word but rather with a story of dreams: "This I saw, and this will take place." Finally he announced that the coming of the Last Judgment would occur within the next year. "As they heard him prophesying with the words, ὡς ὅτι ἐνέστηκεν ἡ ἡμέρα τοῦ κυρίου,[30] they pleaded and prayed to the Lord with great crying and moaning, for day and night they were faced with the immediate coming of the Day of Judgment. Thus out of their great fear and despondency he caused the brothers to abandon their fields and lands, and most of them sold all of their possessions." The bishop even asserted that if the prophecy did not come true, one no longer needed to believe the Holy Scripture.[31] The result was that after a year of futile waiting the bishop was humiliated and ashamed; and the brothers face great vexation for since they have sold all their possessions, they must now go begging.

What should prompt us to interpret the agitation of our letter another way than is presented to us with this story? Why should the preaching of Christ during his day have had less an enthusiastic, heavy, and frightening impact than at the time of the events related above?

The analogy with Hippolytus's story can obviously be further explained. It is clear from our passage that the writer distinguishes between those people who call forth the trepidation from those for whom it has been announced. That results from the structure of the words of 2 Thess 2:3: μή τις ὑμᾶς ἐξαπατήσῃ κατὰ μηδένα τρόπον. But also it can be understood from the statement of 2 Thess 2:2. When the great fright is called forth διὰ πνεύματος, διὰ λόγου, and δι' ἐπιστολῆς ὡς δι' ἡμῶν, so then these are

29. Cf. Bonwetsch, *Studien zu den Kommentaren Hippolytus*, 73ff.; also Harnack, Untitled Entry, *Theologische Literatur*, 36–37.

30. Thus Hippolytus, who could well know what ἐνέστηκεν means, has understood this word in the sense of the immediate imminence (of the Parousia).

31. At the end of this story the following assertion is made: "but the Scriptures appear to be true." Unfortunately Hippolytus does not tell us what role the Scriptures played in regard to the agitation and tumult in Pontus.

certainly people who prove from these authoritative sayings that the Day of Judgment is coming. Thereby each one would be reminded with the διὰ πνεύματος of the dreams and prophesies of the Bishop of Pontus. For it is hardly to be doubted that this phrase is meant to refer to prophetic address. To be sure, one is not dealing with older recorded prophecies but rather with spirited, lively, even echoing prophecies that one has presented here as proof and which one believes. It is also in order here that we encounter the mission of the prophets, for the Day of Judgment belongs especially to their domain.

What actually motivates the writer to oppose these people and to counter the sentiment that they have voiced is not directly alluded to with a definite statement here. Was it only the uproar itself along with the trepidation that prompted him to write this? Or had there already been other episodes and eschatological proclamations that had become perceptible in the life of the community?

Such a question is integrally related to this matter. Also the views of Hippolytus that with their clarity successfully enrich our understanding of the character and development of the possibilities of such movements lead us in this direction. Certainly they should not mislead us to make indefinite analogies. It can only be determined from this letter itself if a close similarity between the earlier and the later events actually exists.

The place to begin is with the section 2 Thess 3:6–15. Almost all exegetes place this passage in the closest relationship to the eschatological theme: the idleness that is rebuked and reprimanded is viewed here as "devout" idleness that accompanies that particular eschatological sentiment.[32]

To some extent one has also observed the same theme in the first letter. But Spitta[33] has contested this view and I believe with the utmost justification. The indication that the idleness about which one is warned has religious origins and reasons is not at all found in the first letter. For although immediately after these words the text speaks of the Parousia, such a definite conclusion is not to be found. The section of 1 Thess 4:13–18 begins with a new theme; but the word, ἡσυχάζειν, is then only to be understood when one juxtaposes against it the disruptiveness of uneasiness, neglect, disorder and pursuit of pleasure. Such a laziness is just as little em-

---

32. Dobschütz, *Die urchristlichen Gemeiden*, 70–71. He has recently advanced this view with a somewhat freer portrayal.

33. Spitta, *Zur Geschichte*, 130ff. Cf. Spitta's following explanation; von Hoffmann, *Die heilige Schrift*, 230–31. He presents a related argument; Zahn, *Einleitung*, 159. He opposes Spitta's conclusion.

barrassing for the formation of a community as the sins that Paul forbids with his call for holiness in 1 Thess 4:1–12. It is just in this context that the admonition is found along with all that Paul adds with regard to this trend that the idleness discredits the community in face of the pagans and that one should not become another's burden as with 1 Thess 4:12. If we had only the first letter, one would hardly at all have arrived at the conclusion to see here evidence for eschatological enthusiasm. Only the second letter points in this direction. Here an abnormal intensification of expectation for the future can be clearly found, and it does not seem to be coincidental that just here the idleness receives a reprimand once more, surely a sharp and pointed one: the pursuit of idleness appears to have received thus justifiable support by means of eschatological enthusiasm and furor.

If the second letter is a pseudepigraphon, so then every thought of a continuity of the relationships ceases to exist. Perhaps there would be some continuity if the composition was relatively early, but certainly such is true if it followed much later and the letter had nothing at all to do with Thessalonica.[34] However that might be, in each case the meaning of 1 Thess 4:11–12 is not pertinent for 2 Thess 3:6–15.

It seems rather awkward to attribute a sermon of punishment and threat to a matter of secondary importance that had nothing to do with the purpose of the letter, if on the contrary judged according to its length and elaboration, it must have been very important for the writer. Yet it would be most unusual where there is such a close relationship as here. Such a correlation seems directly obvious considering the report of Hippolytus about the movement in the city of Pontus. For although the words of his story about the divestiture of possessions and the neglect and disregard of fields definitely offers a different picture than our passage— since in this context the reprehensible ones would not have eaten their own bread, both have the same theme that all care and worry about the earthly life is futile over and against the coming of the Last Judgment. Thus one should seek rather to prepare oneself with listening, teaching, and praying for the coming of the judge.

For all of that, however, it is much more probable that 2 Thess 3:6–15 simply speaks of the "inertia vulgaris."

If our letter is dependent upon the first letter, so it is also true with this passage. The original text can also have been the actual motive that

---

34. Holtzmann, "Zum zweiten Thessalonicherbrief," 102–3. He should well have reached this consequential view of this matter.

compelled the author to take up this theme. But the reason that he took this theme from the section 1 Thess 4:3–12 and then namely so much more thoroughly and urgently than the first letter elaborates upon it can have arisen because he has been confronted in his own community with the harm and detriment caused by those who avoid work and loaf about. A verse such as 2 Thess 3:10, "Whoever does not work should also not eat," is very appropriate for those people who were only vagabonds and nothing more. However, those who believe the message of the nearness of the Last Judgment would not have for the most part been the subjects of this passage, but rather to the contrary those who sought to make themselves comfortable for the coming of the Last Judgment. But then one does not rightly understand the sternness and the abrasiveness of the writer, his threat of disciplinary measures, and the cessation of intercourse. The responsibility for work belonged to the accepted moral code of the early church, but why does the writer not at all move on to the view that the root of this behavior of the ἄτακτοι for the most part lay with religious sentiment? Not one word in this entire section reminds us of the question of eschatology. That in itself is rather unusual. But there is one additional matter—this section that concerns work appears in the letter as an addendum. Namely at the outset originally the writer already wanted to close the letter with the verses of 2 Thess 3:1–5.[35] Yet an additional exposition and discourse is less likely with regard for a view that lay so close to his primary interest, for one that was so basically related.[36] Still, accordingly, one does not recognize any unusual or special impact of fright on the development of the life of the community. Such an element is not a required prerequisite that led the writer to decide to write his letter.

A similar negative result yields itself with other points and aspects of the letter that one could perhaps relate to the eschatological expectation and enthusiasm. Affliction and persecution are mentioned with the introduction. Precisely because this concept leads to a small digression found in 2 Thess 1:5–10 that is not even vaguely similar to that of the first letter and moreover because one may hear a strong element of hate from the words that concern divine revenge, it appears that the writer is dealing here with a theme that was very important for his community. Then the concept that the Lord is returning could easily have arisen through the eruption of a

---

35. Holtzmann, "Zum zweiten Thessalonicherbrief," 78–79. He gives a further explanation here.

36. Von Hoffmann, *Die heilge Schrift*, 364. He has made a similar remark.

persecution.[37] This would have been understood as the beginning of the great θλῖψις.

But it cannot be actually determined if such affliction really existed at that moment. The present tense of ἀνέχεσθε found in 2 Thess 1:4 is not decisive if the letter has derived this concept of affliction from another source. There is absolutely no mention of a sudden and new outbreak of affliction. Particularly one would clearly have to expect that the pinnacle would be broken off of the powerful argument that once lay in affliction itself, if in fact affliction was the real, fertile ground for the ever-growing expectation of the Parousia. The dependence on the first letter alone for such a relationship with the general experiences that one confronted in early and later Christianity will sufficiently explain this passage.

With three words, the writer of 2 Thess 2:2 has designated the authority upon which one has leaned and supported oneself in order to make the immediate nearness of the Last Judgment certain: πνεῦμα, λόγος, and ἐπιστολή. The third element has the addition, ὡς δι' ἡμῶν, that can also belong to λόγος but that has nothing whatsoever to do with πνεῦμα.

The prophets are considered and remembered here. The writer of our letter obviously discredits them such that he as Paul himself—as the apostolic authority—warns the people from their prophecy. Besides the word of the prophets it was Paul himself—the διὰ λόγου is at first omitted here—and certainly a letter from him or perhaps even a series of letters upon which one especially called for authority.

Here I must once more highlight the matter and how it is that one might understand this discussion and the many related expressions if one proceeds on the basis of a Pauline origin of the letter.

The number of possible interpretations is limited from the outset by the closing remark of 2 Thess 3:17–18. If Paul actually makes his own writing the sign or symbol for his letters, he can only have wanted to readily give a means whereby one could recognize authentic Pauline letters from forged and alleged ones. Viewed against the background of all of Paul's letters this one-time mention of the mark or sign is so conspicuous that it alone is enough to arouse a strong suspicion against the authenticity of the letter, especially when no definite source or occasion for it can be assumed. The reason for it could lie with matters that are not known to us. Regarding our letter, however, just such a supposition is not at all satisfying. Since the first letter does not mention anything related to the matter, since only a

---

37. Von Hoffmann has arrived at this same combination of events. Cf. 1 Pet 4:17.

short amount of time lies between the first and second letters, and since no message from Paul will have reached the community during this time, one must perhaps expect a suggestion in which experiences would guide the Apostle to an explanation that would nonetheless be most likely the right conclusion. Such a suggestion was virtually indispensable when the cause for this, which here is certainly the first thought or idea, had to do with something that he himself had heard about Thessalonica.

With regard to this deliberation one must immediately consider it impossible that Paul could have viewed verse 2 Thess 2:2 to be a misunderstanding of his first letter. Therefore with this not seldomly representative, accepted view of the matter, 2 Thess 3:17 forfeits the very motive that could very easily make it understandable. But it is just as awkward to ascribe letters to him with 2 Thess 2:2 that could possibly have been deceptively attributed to him. For then 2 Thess 3:17 would be supported by the assertion of 2 Thess 2:2. Yet if that were so, we understand even less what might have brought Paul precisely at this moment to think and ponder so earnestly over this possibility. This is to say then that 2 Thess 3:17 as well as 2 Thess 2:2 would remain misunderstood. Moreover, precisely for 2 Thess 2:2 the reference to the fragmentary knowledge about the experiences of the Apostle during that time would be least of all appropriate.[38] The thought of a possible forgery with this verse could not merely in general have come into consideration here except for one most definite question. The thought of a possible forgery must have been motivated by some kind of event.

Paul can only have had one opinion as he wrote the words of 2 Thess 2:2 and then followed them with 2 Thess 3:17. He states clearly that a letter with this (eschatological) instruction had been deceptively attributed to him, one that he did not approve of.

Certainly the disclosure is also logically possible that one is dealing here with a letter that has been mistakenly attributed to Paul without any deceptive intent of the author.[39] Assuming that Paul knew this, then the remark of his with 2 Thess 3:17 would not be groundless. Yet alone as a factual matter this explanation is not satisfactory, for one comes to the view that it has been reached as a matter of necessity. Letters of antiquity tend to say exactly at the beginning from whom they have come. How then could

---

38. Bornemann, *Die Thessalonicherbriefe*, 467, 536. His comments exaggerate this skepticism.

39. Cf. von Hoffmann z. St.; Bleek-Mangold, *Einleitung*, 451. Especially the comment made by Mangold. (Bleek himself thinks of a misunderstanding of the first letter, and can therefore only give an extremely weak and lackluster explanation of 2 Thess 3:17.)

one consider Paul to be the author?[40] Obviously one must proceed to the very dubious assumption of a letter without a heading,[41] and then of course the mistake would be highly improbable and curious. Such an arbitrary letter could not so easily have been assumed to be one of Paul's letters. Furthermore how could Paul have viewed it as anything other than a forgery, if he knew of such a letter that had been attributed to him. One would then have to presume with a new approach that he had learned from whom the letter had been sent and what kind of person this was. Yet, on the contrary, the actual writer had remained unknown even in Thessalonica!

If one modifies this version just as Zahn[42] has attempted, then the "quirky subtleness" is not at all eliminated or reduced. Particularly the advantage that 2 Thess 3:17 remains understandable is completely lost once more. Zahn considers it most probable that "(oral and) written messages and letters from the surrounding area have reached Thessalonica. Because of their origin and without any deceptive purpose from the people who might have sent them, these writings and messages have called forth the mistake that this view of the Day of the Lord was grounded and based on the authority of Paul (i.e., Paul, Silvanus, and Timothy)." If according to the written letters and messages it can be concluded that they originated with the intent of the Apostle, then 2 Thess 3:17 actually remains completely unexplained.[43] This verse offers us nothing specific for an appraisal of the opinions that would clarify his purpose, for it explains then only a relation-

---

40. Cf. Spitta, *Zur Geschichte*, 152.

41. Von Hoffmann actually proceeds on the basis of a letter without a name.

42. Zahn, *Einleitung*, 167.

43. Admittedly Zahn finds a way. He remarks: "But since Paul views various and very different ways of such deception as possible for the future (2 Thess 2:3 κατὰ μηδένα τρόπον), so then it was absolutely required to point out and make clear that only letters that were sent directly from him and which were marked by the signature of his own greeting should be considered as a valid expression of his own opinion (2 Thess 3:17)." Therefore the following is asserted: 1) Since one has obtained a false understanding of his opinion and view from assertions made by those in his surroundings, Paul has come to understand the possibility of more falsifications later in the future. 2) Paul intends to confront the possibility of later falsifications with his explanation given in 2 Thess 3:17 that his letters are to be acknowledged always by the signature of this own hand. At the same time Paul wants with this same explanation (this appears to be somewhat contrived for the Apostle who is always very busy and expressive, see above) to emphasize the fact that only his own letters and not those from the surrounding area are to be recognized and considered as a valid expression of his opinion. (Without this observation then the actual event of 2 Thess 2:2 concerning the "possibility" of 2 Thess 2:3 would be thoroughly forgotten) Zahn places considerable demands here on the imagination of his readers.

The Authenticity of the Second Letter to the Thessalonians

ship to 2 Thess 2:2 when Paul himself might appear to be the originator of the written letters. Still there is another difficulty with the assumption that the letters of such content should have originated in or have come from Paul's surrounding.

The argument remains with the realization that if Paul wrote 2 Thess 2:2 and 2 Thess 3:17, then he thought that his name had been misused for the forgery. The question can only be the following: Was this actually the case or was he mistaken about it?

If such is true, there arises the very stark difficulty that Paul does not take the occasion to properly denounce, but rather is satisfied only to mention the forged letter along with others. Nevertheless, if he believed that such an unusual incident had taken place, he must have been absolutely appalled by it, and doubly so, because the misuse of his name had given rise to a view and sentiment that he disapproved of. Moreover the matter does not get any better when one presumes that there is inadequate instruction concerning the "what" and the "how"; or that because of the convoluted and confused report that has come to him, the Apostle only suspects a forgery. Then there would have been the question and even the demand for further letters and correspondence as with the explanation of 2 Thess 3:17.

This difficulty only increases if one is actually dealing here with a blatant forgery. The supporters of this view have for the most part missed the skepticism that they have so substantially called upon to counter the possibility that our letter was deceptively attributed to Paul at a much later time. Did it occur, for example, during the life of Paul, at a time when his relationship to the community was new and in an early stage; and yet he did not at all bother to write another letter using his name and hope that it would be accordingly acknowledged? One should, by all means, concede the impossibility of such a perception.

The presupposition alone that Paul has mistakenly assumed a forgery is also not more believable, for it really shifts the offense over one further point. According to Spitta and Jülicher Paul has heard that on the basis of a letter from him that someone has reported the alarming eschatological proclamation to the community. The first reference of 1 Thess 5:1–11 is the source of this report. But Paul did not really arrive at the thought that someone has misunderstood him. As Jülicher says, "This mistake thoroughly explains 2 Thess 2:2 as well as 2 Thess 3:17."[44] This is admitted, but if

---

44. Jülicher, *Einleitung*, 41–48.

only his mistake itself were explained for us![45] It is certainly true that with regard to related matters we easily overlook the obvious possibilities, but still we would not like to appeal to such a vexatious experience regarding this possibility. Rather we must burden the account of the poor, innocent messenger, whom one detects from 2 Thess 3:11,[46] and attribute to him extremely confused discourses in order to tolerably understand why it is that Paul with reference to the obvious does not come to the thought about his own letter. But then the question itself remains unresolved. Without definite facts, how could he easily be certain about it rather than suspect a forgery and make a request concerning it? But of no lesser importance another question: how did it come about that the man who carried so perfectly in memory all the content of his earlier letter, and precisely then, when others reminded him, no longer knew that he had written something about the meaning of the prediction and prophecy about the coming of the Last Judgment that one could only misunderstand?[47]

Only more deleterious matters arise when the words διὰ λόγου are considered and observed. Such occurs when one likewise places the ὡς δι' ἡμῶν next to διὰ λόγου just as to δι'ἐπιστολῆς. It is most unlikely, however, that the phrase, διὰ λόγου, could be a completely separate element. From the διὰ πνεύματος that stands solely on its own,[48] it follows that nothing at all can be concluded, nothing for or against the arguments at hand. For it is not easier to place a phrase with the addendum δι' ἡμῶν next to two independent phrases as to combine two phrases with the addendum to another phrase that is without an addendum. And if the Apostle wanted to name a putative word or message from him or an alleged letter of his along with the spirit, so there is nothing to be objected to against this kind of expression. But the following comments speak and argue against the independence of the phrase, διὰ λόγου. 1) If λόγος, the quiet and sober discourse, is to be

---

45. Spitta, *Zur Geschichte*, 152–53. He makes the attempt at this.

46. Spitta, *Zur Geschichte*. ἀκούομεν γάρ τινας περιπατοῦντας ἐν ὑμῖν ἀτάκτως. Spitta refers also to 1 Thess 3:5.

47. Jülicher, *Einleitung*, 47. On page 47 of the new edition of his introduction to the New Testament Jülicher even assumes that with regard to the compositional conception of the second letter Paul has called to mind and remembers exactly what he wrote and perhaps earlier orally reported to the community, particularly the primary assertion of his view. Yet despite all this there is an error and misunderstanding?

48. Bornemann z. St.; Hoffmann, *Die heilige Schrift*. Both Bornemann and Hoffmann do not join ὡς δι'ἡμῶν with διὰ λόγου; Zahn, *Einleitung*, 166. However Zahn proceeds with the opposite alternative and combines them.

viewed as the intellectual explanation and proclamation in the meetings of the community as opposed to the charismatic utterance of the message of prophecy[49]—and here one can hardly think of anything else—then the additions such as σοφίας, διδαχῆς, and γνώσεως are hardly dispensable.[50] 2) When a few verses later (2 Thess 2:15) the usage, εἴτε διὰ λόγου εἴτε δι'ἐπιστολῆς ἡμῶν, is found, then this is a parallel which has a strong and definite significance. 3) One could add with regard to a third comment that the mere word, λόγος, that has as much authority as πνεῦμα or even an apostolic letter, cannot be disregarded; but on the contrary that is an uncertain reflection.

The Apostle seems to assume not only that a letter has been falsely attributed to him but also that a word or words have been imputed to him which one has spread abroad pertaining to the eschatological question. If this is actually his opinion, so the matter becomes even more puzzling when he slurs and glides so quickly and calmly over such things. Furthermore we must double either the audacity of the manipulation against him or the oddity of his misunderstanding. Thus, because he believes to know for certain about the forged letter and merely suspects the imputation of words to him or considers such possible, should he therefore from the very beginning want to refrain from making his own comments from his point of view? It is not at all clear to me that someone who knew about a definite letter falsely attributed to him would then take in hand his own defense and clearance in such a way that he places on the same level both the mere possibilities alongside the definite facts.

The more precisely one follows the different suggestions, the clearer it becomes that the defenders of the Pauline origin of this letter regarding this point entangle themselves in the utmost difficulties that they perhaps lessen with their appeal and recourse to uncontrollable possibilities clouded by the unknown but which they nonetheless are not able to eliminate. Those who are a bit naïve and impartial may have been able to bring these difficulties better to light. But as we have stated above, it is actually this point viewed secondarily alongside the primary argument that is the most important determinant that can be voiced against the authenticity of the letter.

49. Bornemann z. St.

50. Tertullian, *De Resurrectione Carnis*, chapter 24. Tertullian further elaborates with a discussion or sermon (perhaps also via the spirit?): *scilicet pseudoprophetarum*. A "*scilicet pseudapostolorum*" corresponds then and accords via "*epistolam*" to that previous expression.

Objections to an Early Fiction

Let us return now to our comprehensive study. If a later writer speaks here and addresses his letter with the destination for Thessalonica, so from the beginning no assumption is more probable than that with the words, δι' ἐπιστολῆς ὡς δι' ἡμῶν, somehow the First Letter to the Thessalonians has been denoted. This assumption will be attested by means of a further analysis, and from this point we arrive at the idea and concept that has already resulted from other considerations[51] that 2 Thess 2 has the eschatological assertions of the first letter in view. The expression itself, however, does not speak of a definite letter as the genus ἐπιστολή occurs next to the genus λόγος. Therefore when it can be factually justified to consider still other letters next to the First Letter to the Thessalonians, so then the expression would not stand in the way of that. But despite the indefiniteness, it allows also for the assumption that only one letter is to be considered, even the letter to that community to which the writer himself purports to address with his comments.[52] I can name the genre if I only have an example in mind. For the time being, let us remain with this presupposition.

Should the First Letter to the Thessalonians be considered suspicious by the writer and pushed aside as non-Pauline? The first impression of the addendum, ὡς δι' ἡμῶν, in conjunction with the closing remark of 2 Thess 3:17 will easily direct our consideration to this view that has been advanced by Hilgenfeld.[53] The factual relationship of the eschatology of the second letter to the first letter certainly does not stand in the way of this. Yet this view cannot be substantiated. 2 Thess 2:15 is certainly the message of the first letter, and so the authority of even our doubtful letter would thus immediately be formally recognized. Furthermore, how would it come about that the writer does not proceed with a sense of propriety and repeat many of the associations and expressions of the first letter? Above all, our letter simply assumes with its formluations the reputable appearance of the first letter that the writer could hardly have the intent to want to uproot with just half of a stroke of the pen.[54]

When the first letter is not contested, it appears to be a matter of its perception or of a misunderstanding of its instruction. The writer would

---

51. See 43–44 above.

52. One can here as little as with 2 Thess 2:15 stipulate that the article then must come before ἐπιστολῆς.

53. Hilgenfeld, *Einleitung*, 646; Unitled Entry, *Zeitschrift*, 249. Cf. Rauch, Untitled Entry, *Zeitschrift*, 463; Holtzmann, *Einleitung*, 214, 16.

54. Zahn, *Einleitung*, 176. He develops a related interpretation.

want to make it clear with the words, ὡς δι' ἡμῶν, that he has not expressed the words and message of the letter with the assumed meaning given for them and has not written them. For example it might thus be rewritten: "as if we had wanted to say (with word and letter)."[55] Yet solely on its own the grammar has placed a stone in the way and has ruled out this possibility. The contradiction of the putative and alleged over against the actuality that would be referred to here with ὡς δι' ἡμῶν can only reflect the very word and letter itself, not something that one has found in it. But if one wants to combine the διὰ before ἡμῶν with θροεῖσθαι rather than ἐπιστολῆς, that also does not help. For in any case λόγος and ἐπιστολή definitely receive again their completion and correlation through the δι' ἡμῶν that makes their mention in this context actually understandable.

With this insight Schmiedel[56] meant that a letter falsely attributed to Paul has surfaced that emphasized the nearness of the Parousia much more strongly than 1 Thess 5:2; 4:15, or that the writer has deceptively invented this. Yet each of these disclosures certainly pay much too dearly for the correct grammar. For if something with reference to the non-Pauline origin of our letter is at all possible, then it must be something that is related to the First Letter to the Thessalonians. Actually all depends on this matter for the understanding of the entire second letter, as it will be clearly shown.[57] This definite point would be truly abandoned with the first assumption and would thus favor one of the most questionable opinions. But the second attributes the writer with a fiction that either would have had no purpose at all or one that was more than improbable. The intent[58] of our writer to ensure and prepare for the affirmation of the authenticity of his letters with 2 Thess 3:17[59] does not truly allow for anything other than the attempt to discredit the first letter. How? Should the fear of a distrustful reception of the explanation of 2 Thess 3:17, one that he has still not given, an explanation

---

55. Cf. Reuss, *Geschichte*, 74: "as though I myself had taught you that which now frightens you." (But Reuss considers the letter to be authentic.)

56. Schmiedel, Untitled Entry, *Handkommentar*, 9–37. He takes up 2 Thess 2:2.

57. Holtzmann, "Zum zweiten Thessalonicherbrief," 105. He states the following: "One interpretative hypothesis of the riddle of the second letter must above all virtually give consideration and do justice to its alternative character."

58. Schmiedel, Untitled Entry, *Handkommentar*, 37. According to Schmiedel there should be the additional intention to refer to and emphasize the importance of his writing.

59. Holtzmann, "Zum zweiten Thessalonikerbrief," 107. Holtzmann asserts that 2 Thess 3:17 "has already well been prepared by 2 Thess 2:2."

that itself has only the purpose to confront this mistrust, have accompanied him throughout this entire letter; and should this fear in and of itself have led him to the distant thought of an earlier falsely attributed letter, one that is extremely clever because it was brought about by the calculated brevity of the hastily conceived comment of 2 Thess 2:2? That is an inconceivable chain of thoughts for a Christian of the first century, unless we would want to endow him with the most refined and subtle psychology of a modern intellectual. Besides, the expression διὰ λόγου remains unexplained with this view.

But we need not at all be subject to the acceptance of such questionable assumptions. There is a possible interpretation and analysis that does not force the grammar and that is factually satisfactory. Kern has already presented this,[60] and very clearly, but perhaps not quite clearly enough for it has not made a large and definite impression.

Just as because the question concerning falsely attributed letters has directly played a role in the biblical criticism of this letter irrespective of 2 Thess 2:2 and because the writer must somehow to the contrary disclaim the prevailing importance of "spirit," "word," and "letter," so certainly the impression easily arises as whether or not the ὡς must refer to something that is only assumed but which is not really the case. But that is only a preconception. For such a supposition that is given with our "as if," does not occur at all with ὡς. The ὡς expresses essentially only a subjective relationship. This can consist of a negation of an objective statement but by no means is this required. When the parable of the unjust landlord states: διεβλήθη αὐτῷ (i.e., the Lord) ὡς διασκορπίζων τά ὑπάρχοντα αὐτοῦ, so the ὡς does not reveal anything at all about the truth or the falsehood of the blatancy.[61] But when, for example, Paul with 1 Cor 7:25 writes: γνώμην δὲ δίδωμι ὡς ἠλεημένος ὑπὸ κυρίου πιστὸς εἶναι, so everyone knows that the ὡς does not detract and discount anything from the reality of the experienced pardon and expresses the view that the Apostle is also aware of this. Here with our verse the ὡς does not even in any way abrogate the view that the verse actually deals with the word and letter of the Apostle, and just as little does it provide any doubt about the interpretation of these matters. Much more as Kern states, it suggests "only the attributed and appropriated

---

60. Kern, "Über 2 Thess 2:1–12," 149. One should not place Kern's view alongside that of Reuss as has often occurred. They are surely synonymous but they are grounded in a very different and divergent exegesis.

61. Jülicher, *Die Gleichnisreden Jesu*, 496. Jülicher has rightly characterized this translation as imprudent: "as if he had denigrated his wealth and property."

mission of the Apostle to the others." Just as the Apostle has preached and written, so one has made this effective and appropriate for the eschatological theme; and precisely because his authority has been given and established, one has become on the other hand very frightened. A mere μήτε διὰ λόγου μήτε δι'ἐπιστολῆς δι' ἡμῶν[62] would mean that one would actually become frightened because of the word and letter of the Apostle, but that thereby one should not allow oneself be frightened. A ὡς before δι' ἡμῶν fully allows for just such a thought, but further adds the relationship of the opinion of the ones who are frightened that the letter, even though it comes from the Apostle, gives the basis for the belief for the coming of the Day of the Lord as well as the fright and tumult. Therefore one should translate as follows: "neither by word nor further by letter but rather from us." One could rewrite it as follows: do not allow yourselves to become frightened because someone has made the word and letter from me to be effectively applicable, for both have come from me. Regarded then from the writer's point of view and also with this assertion, a feeling of his dignity and esteem becomes evident (i.e., truly an expression about the reputation of Paul). This aspect of the matter is even less obvious for one who has acted out the role of Paul than the commanding and authoritative tone in 2 Thess 3 that one has often sensed.

Clearly we are returning in a completely different manner to the opinion that the writer implies that they have falsely interpreted the first letter. He does not say that himself; but he also does not say—one must observe the parallel— that the "spirit" whose dictums and assertions one listens to might not actually be spirit.[63] Yet when he explains that they should not become frightened by what he has said or written, so therefore surely it is meant tacitly yet nonetheless expressed distinctly that he has interpreted and meant the spoken and written words differently than they have understood them—and rightly so since then the authentic instruction from 2 Thess 2:3–12 is immediately presented and follows in the text, from which

---

62. 2 Thess 2:15 reads as follows: κρατεῖτε τὰς παραδόσεις ἃς ἐδιδάχθητε εἴτε διὰ λόγου εἴτε δι' ἐπιστολῆς ἡμῶν. According to our interpretation this verse occurs most surely and clearly in a relationship to 2 Thess 2:2. Cf. Kern, "Über 2 Thess 2:1–12," 150.

63. Spiritual authority and apostolic authority are evaluated somewhat differently in this document insofar as the former is not even recognized in the existing case while the latter is acknowledged but has been denied its proper use and understanding. As for the warning that one should not allow oneself to become frightened, both occur however in the same logical relationship.

the proper understanding of the misunderstood words has been derived and formulated.

From my perception this obviously accepted manner of expression would be unusual and curious for Paul. He is compelled to feel much too identified and personally associated with his earlier writing such that he becomes too concerned for the uniformity of his opinion. Therefore, he can only say so drearily, objectively, and so negatively that one should not allow oneself to become frightened on the basis of his letter or a letter sent from him.[64] On the other hand, it sounds appropriate in the mouth of a Pseudo-Paulus who superbly pretends to be the writer of this letter to the Thessalonians, but who is not capable of genuine feeling. He simply faces the fact that one has led not only the word of the spirit but also the Pauline statements and their meaning into the fray as false and dangerous proclamations. This fact strictly and simply accords with his warning: the apostolic message and utterance is for him something even objective, something that lies outside himself just like the discourses and message of the prophets. Perhaps it becomes a bit clearer when I say merely the following: here the manner of speech becomes apparent, such a manner that a writer would choose when without his Pauline mask he wanted to oppose and confront the authority of his opponents: Do not call upon and rely on the spirit or the Apostle Paul!

The μή τις ὑμᾶς ἐξαπατήσῃ, 2 Thess 2:3, prepares the way for this interpretation that with one stroke sets one free from all former tortuous attempts, and from the δι' ἐπιστολῆς δι' ἡμῶν derives the actual facts without difficulty. Moreover, without falsifying the purpose one could appear to mislead and to deceive and thus pretend that the deceptive element lies within the disputed opinion itself: that teaching that is not the "truth" is certainly deception and allurement. Perhaps here one will seek to oppose us with the view taken above[65] that 2 Thess 3:17 loses its point if Paul considers 2 Thess 2:2 to be a misunderstanding. By itself, however, this can only be the case when the authentic Paul is writing 2 Thess 3:17. But with a false Paul 2 Thess 3:17 can be thoroughly explained on the basis of the motive to put the valid Pauline stamp on the falsely attributed letter. Thus there is no need of such a purpose to warn others from falsifications. Here 2 Thess 3:17 has nothing at all to do with 2 Thess 2:2.

---

64. Once more the objection and doubt arise that 2 Thess 3:17 may be intended as a riddle and mystery.

65. See 53 above.

The Authenticity of the Second Letter to the Thessalonians

Finally, what is the meaning of λόγος when placed alongside ἐπιστολή? In the middle of the exposition about the Anti-Christ in 2 Thess 2:5 we find the following expression: Οὐ μνημονεύετε ὅτι ἔτι ὢν πρὸς ὑμᾶς ταῦτα ἔλεγον ὑμῖν.[66] From our point of view this can only have one meaning: the writer legitimizes all that he has presented and declaimed as Pauline with this special phrase. Paul has actually stated orally all that he did not write in the First Letter to the Thessalonians during his visit and stay in Thessalonica long ago. But that is certainly not so subtly conceived as it might appear. For the remembrance of the time in Thessalonica has been attributed to the writer by means of the first letter which speaks at length about this not only with 1 Thess 3:4 but also with 1 Thess 2:1–16; 4:1–2, 6, 11; 5:2. Accordingly one will find first of all with the διὰ λόγου of 2 Thess 2:2 a similar retrospection about the past, the time of the oral mission and discourse just as it is recorded with ἔλεγον with 2 Thess 2:5. Then it would have obviously been faked and mistakenly reported that Paul has made public, oral proclamations just as even so his letter reported unrealistically very early on false and precipitous expectations about the future. But with regard to this because πνεῦμα and ἐπιστολή are not mere words of fictional importance, it thus seems likely that one should consider another possibility.

Should the expression of this passage imply in this regard that with the debate about the eschatological question one did not only speak about letters or a letter from the Apostle but also about his words? Then to be sure it would have been meant with the written text that the spoken word and written letter were only formally distinguished from one another, for

---

66. If this verse could have been written by Paul, then one must make the following assumptions: 1) As Paul comes to speak about the χρόνοι καὶ καιροί in 1 Thess 5:1–11, he does not remember his earlier teachings about the Anti-Christ. That was the topic on page 45 above. 2) But at least some of the Thessalonians obviously remember very little as well if anything at all about this, and that is even more remarkable. Their knowledge (or rather their lack of it) does not prevent them from arriving at the understanding that the day of the Parousia already stands before the door and from interpreting the passage of 1 Thess 5:1–11 against Paul's intent and purpose (if one is permitted to presuppose that 2 Thess 2: 1–12 is alluded to with this section of the first letter). 3) Paul has already taught in Thessalonica everything that he at first explained and dealt with, but now he is not satisfied to make do with that such that he proceeds to proclaim everything once more, as if it were happening for the first time. Thus it is presupposed that the ταῦτα of 2 Thess 2:5 does not need to be limited to the content of 2 Thess 2:3–4 (This interpretation is clearly only possible if the νῦν of 2 Thess 2:6 does not stand in opposition to ἔτι ὢν πρὸς ὑμᾶς. More about this below 107–108). If one then brings the οἴδατε of 2 Thess 2:6 into the discussion, so it may be assumed that at the time Paul is writing, the readers are already familiar with the teaching which he previously proclaimed. (Cf. 108 Anm 1.)

they created a kind of logical hendiadys.⁶⁷ But the parallel verse of 2 Thess 2:15 does not support this viewpoint. Considered alone, this verse sounds very different. Yet the assumption that the existing separation of word and letter of 2 Thess 2:15 is only a consequence of the schema used in 2 Thess 2:2 is hardly tenable and certainly cannot be proved. Διὰ λόγου in 2 Thess 2:2 has been written thus with regard to the relationship of Paul's oral and public mission for the community. This phrase is then meaningless for the actual motive and occasion for the letter. The λόγος used by Paul alongside his use of πνεῦμα and ἐπιστολή does not designate any tangible importance. However, perhaps one can find a definite difficulty with this interpretation. But I am not aware of any perception and view of διὰ λόγου that did not also retain this great difficulty. On the other hand, the expression itself as used in this verse with the other two words is by no means incomprehensible. The writer, prompted by the word usage of the first letter, has obviously associated himself in this regard with Paul's actual situation. The parallels of 2 Thess 2:5, 15; 3:6, 10 give evidence of this.

It is my view that I have thoroughly explained 2 Thess 2:2 with these comments. Only one other matter requires a word of explanation. Whoever considers our letter not to be authentic must assume that the writer has provided an earlier setting for those things that he himself has experienced and that have motivated him to write, placing them back into Paul's time.⁶⁸ This assumption could perhaps raise some doubt. But considered on its own there is no real difficulty with this view. It was rather natural for the writer to place the mention of unrealistic and enthusiastic expectations for the future in the mouth of Paul, as soon as the Apostle's letter to the Thessalonians was exploited by his opponents to their advantage, and he himself wanted to speak to them as Paul with a new letter to the Thessalonians. With this dating of the letter back into the time of those events he has done nothing more than any other writers of fictional letters have always done. He has also written nothing that would suggest to his readers the thought of a forgery or that would have given rise to the worry of the discovery of his forgery. The fact that Paul mentioned his letter and spoke of the agitation and disconcertment of his readers documented by it could not have sounded peculiar or curious to them, for they even called on Paul's letter for their clamorous point of view or knew of such references. Should one find it

---

67. 2 Thess 3:14 would be related to this: Εἰ δέ τις οὐχ ὑπακούει τῷ λόγῳ ἡμῶν διὰ τῆς ἐπιστολῆς.

68. See n. 41 above.

objectionable that precisely now in the present as well as back in the time of Paul the divination of prophets had announced and proclaimed the nearness of the Day of the Lord? Was the "spirit" thus not surely and naturally on the agenda when one was dealing with the secrets of the future?

Let us recapitulate. Our letter has resulted from the following situation.

Somewhere the view has been formulated that the long-awaited Day of the Lord has really drawn near. Several people overwhelm the masses with this belief, and they have made a definite impression. Consternation and fright come to the fore. To what extent definite things reveal the actual coming of the Lord's Day has not been reported to us. Prophecies and revelations played an important role. Supposedly it was precisely the bearers of the movement themselves who prophesized and relied on dreams and visions. But then alongside these prophecies Paul himself is especially called to the forefront. What he says is not merely the word of an arbitrary person but the authoritative word of the Apostle. Here it seems entirely possible that one has not limited oneself to the proclamations of one letter (Cf. 1 Cor 15:51–52; 7:29).[69] But one has laid a finger on one letter in particular (i.e., on the passage from 1 Thessalonians 5). This can be presupposed by means of coincidental reasons. A passage more distinctive and better disposed for the imminent Parousia was hardly to be found among all of Paul's letters.

Meanwhile there was no lack of a counter movement. One of the more sober ones who particularly sensed the dangerous and confusing aspects of the enthusiastic, unrealistic, eschatological message—we have no reason to label him a Pauline Christian[70] for the Pauline mask does not make him Pauline—attempts to refute the positon of the opposition by means of a letter written in the name of Paul, thus invoking the authority of Paul. Paul is thus presented to the readers, but the writer himself must provide valid interpretation. Yet nothing compels us to believe that the writer against his own conscience intended to replace or counter Paul's teaching with this self-interpretation. He also has the authority of Paul. When he writes and develops his viewpoint, he has the opinion that he properly understands Paul with regard to this argument and thus seeks to assist Paul's traditional understanding.

It is completely understandable that such a letter was sent to a specific community. As a matter of fact one will not attempt to refer to or compare

---

69. Cf. n. 60 above.

70. Hilgenfeld, *Einleitung*, 651; Kern, "Über 2 Thess 2:1–12," 214; Schmiedel, Untitled Entry, *Handkommentar*, 11–13.

our letter to the apocryphal document, 3 Corinthians, or to the Letter to the Laodicians, for they do not actually present any real parallels. But one may point arguably to the composition of Paul's other letters. One of the obvious characteristics of Paul's letters is that they were intended for definite communities. So the emulation and forgery was from this point of view most natural. But since one dealt here especially with eschatological statements and proclamations, so the writer chose for his composition the form and model of a letter to Thessalonica. Thus it was for the very same people for whom the misinterpreted passage was intended and with an almost marked and definite relationship to the 2 Thess 2:1 that "Paul" thus provided the authentic elucidation and on the basis of which the Parousia was postponed.

Certainly this explanation leaves us with the thought and possibility that the κατέχων can perhaps be very quickly overcome (i.e., that the Anti-Christ can thus be defeated very soon by the sudden appearance of Christ himself). Yet to emphasize this would only mean that one would attribute to the writer consequences that are opposed to his practical tendency and agenda. He does not want at all to counter the belief in an early Parousia from an indefinite and indeterminate sense, and he lets this be known. His concern is rather with the belief in an imminent and immediate Parousia, and his aim is to eliminate the reason for the present unrest and tumult. If with his view one believes that Christ cannot come before the Anti-Christ has been here on earth and that meanwhile the Anti-Christ is to linger and stay, then he has successfully achieved everything that he wants to accomplish for the present time. He has won time, and the fever and fervor of the expectation have been controlled. For the time period under the circumstances to which our letter belongs and when the Parousia has been delayed and postponed, one may presuppose the belief that it is not very far away. The Gospels and other writings offer evidence of this.

It is my opinion that no one will oppose the view[71] that already in a relative early time an all too fiery and fervid expectation for the future could find and encounter definite opposition. With Paul, however, one must confront two matters. Certainly during a very early period one prolonged the perspective for the future and probably not always simply out of the obvious need (i.e., because the Parousia did not come).[72] At any rate the tumultuous enthusiasm, especially when it became acute, will have at all these times have found its opponents. On the other hand, it is self-explanatory

---

71. Bahnsen, Untitled Entry, *Jahrbucher*, 703. He finds this assumption very dubious.
72. Cf. for example Mark 13:10.

that a burning expectation for the future during a relatively advanced time after Paul could not have astonished and provided estrangement, and any further word about that is not required.

All things considered, one certainly cannot presume that the purpose of the writer is perhaps incomprehensible with respect to the assumption of a later composition and that the situation itself is not clear and realistic. Admittedly, we do not learn very much about the details, and especially the historical context to which the reported situation belongs is not very clear to us.

I do not simply mean that we are not able to give a definite place for the situation and that we do not know to what extent the generally propagated extremes of the eschatological controversy appear and develop.[73] Above all I am also referring to the role that Paul or Paul's letters play with regard to this matter.

The letter itself—and with it lies a part of the historical interest that this little document lays claim to—leads us back to that moment of time in which Paul is the authority but, nevertheless, when the reputation of his letters has become to some extent bothersome and disagreeable. A few comments about that matter may be added at this juncture.

Not without justification one has stated that the dogmatic authority of "the Apostle" during the first period of its formation denoted solely an ideal, uncontested, and uncontrollable canon.[74] But for Paul such an assessment must be considerably qualified. The church did not have any written traditions from the other apostles, for they were built up over the years. To the contrary, the Apostle Paul lived on with his letters. Thus always as he belonged to "the Apostles," so too his letters had to have authoritative repute. The authority that designated Paul could therefore not simply arise from the vague concept of all things apostolic, for that which remained of the historical Paul had to be codeterminant with his written legacy. That would

---

73. Holtzmann, "Zum zweiten Thessalonicherbrief," 107–8. He places the letter in a series of multiple, proven attempts to placate and comfort those agitated by the delay of the Parousia by means of postponing the expected date and thus so to strengthen the weary and exhausted hope. But 2 Thess 2:1–3 does not stand in accord and agreement with such a view (Cf. 41. 47 above). Holtzmann himself speaks of "apocalyptic uproar and agitation" on pages 102–3, i.e., he creates a prerequisite that does not allow itself to be reconciled with the point of view presented above. (Holtzmann, *Lehrbuch*, 191. Also with reference to 2 Thess 2:3–12 he speaks of the shimmering and shining tendency to lend the preaching of the Parousia the characteristic of an ongoing and sustained call for alarm.)

74. Weiss, *Einleitung*, 34; Jülicher, *Einleitung*, 286, 376.

be of little importance if one had only considered from a very general point of view that Paul was, for his time, actually what his letters said he was. But his letters stated and reported all kinds of things, and moreover not necessarily anything that was particular and definite. It was only important that over time certain concepts, themes, or pictures of Paul were created from his letters—yet not from his letters alone, but then again not without them, and as such they became historically operative. Likewise this also occurred with the other great personalities and fathers of the history of church doctrine. The name "Paul" came to designate a definite religious or ecclesiastical position, but here he denoted one position and there another. In truth, there were many different Pauls, actually different but more or less true and distinct images and views of him. If the primary vesture of the pastoral letters is not mere coincidence, as I believe, so then the Paul of these letters is the enemy of heresy, the patron of sound, orthodox doctrine, and church polity.

Over and against this Paul of orthodoxy we must differentiate clearly from a completely different Paul as described by Marcion, the enemy of Judaism, the Law, and the Old Testament. Then too according to our letter we might have, once more, an entirely different Paul. For here Paul would be the exponent of boisterous and impetuous eschatological expectation, and with this letter the most important element would be his comments about the end of time. Or are we exaggerating a matter here that is simply irrelevant? Did one occasionally refer to and rely on Paul because just at that time it was expedient and comfortable to do so, even when there was no distinctive understanding of him? Where our letter so deliberately puts Paul in the foreground, it seems rather obvious that the argument about the authority of Paul is not merely a secondary matter. With the premise of the eruption of such eschatological expectation that we find here, it is clear that such thoughts and considerations had already strongly surfaced along this lines. Then they would very probably have been especially fed by Paul's letters. But that is certainly everything that we can suspect and the most that we can sense. This Paulinismus—when we may actually refer to it as such—remains for us an isolated factum. If it actually had a far-reaching meaning and prominence and what that might have been, we simply do not know.

Regardless, it is a matter of interest to see here that the propagation and the esteem of Paul's letters had already very early on generated difficulties for the church. They contained much that had to be reenvisioned or laboriously re-interpreted when it was taken up and explicated. During his lifetime Marcion assuredly drove his opponents sometimes into the corner with the Pauline texts and forced from them artificial interpretatons. It would have been a similar matter with genuine Gnostics. Two passages of the New Testament itself grant us short glimpses into the complete, buried, and oldest history of the letters of Paul in its entirety, a history that most certainly early on flows together with the history of the other authoritative scriptures. These passages might be touched on here briefly.

The first also deals remarkably with eschatology. It is taken from 2 Pet 3:16. When the writer here accuses his opponents—for these must be the ἀμαθεῖς and ἀστήρικτοι and not merely the weak and uneducated or uninformed Christians[75]—with the allegation that they distort definite words of Paul and he himself labels these words "difficult to understand" (δυσνόητα), so one may readily clarify the true meaning of this "difficult to understand" by means of the word, "uncomfortable." The fact that these verses deal with eschatology follows by way of the context. When with 2 Pet 3:15 Paul must come forth as a witness for the concept that the delay of the Parousia can be explained on the basis of the patience of the Lord but that nevertheless wishes the salvation for all (cf. 2 Pet 3:9), so it is also possible for 2 Pet 3:16 to refer to the eschatological question[76] for the sake of which the entire letter has been written.[77] What then was it that may appear to the writer in Paul's letters to be rather dark, misunderstood, and in need of interpretation as he seeks to strengthen the confidence in the Parousia against a radical doubt concerning it? Was it perhaps precisely those verses in which Paul himself hopes to experience the Parousia, verses that certainly counter the concept and thought of a long-suffering delay of the Parousia? This question is not easily answered, and so it can be left open here.

The second verse is taken from the passage about salvation in Jas 2:14–26. In many respects despite the alluring hypothesis of Spitta[78] according to which the letter is not of Christian origin but rather was originally Jewish, I am rather certain that the writer here is looking back to Pauline phrases and expressions along with Pauline reasoning. But it seems to me that there is a misunderstanding when one takes the view that he wanted to oppose Paul. However, it is most likely that at first he did not deal with Paul but rather

---

75. Cf. 2 Pet 3:16: πρὸς τὴν ἰδίαν αὐτῶν ἀπώλειαν. Also especially 2 Pet 3:17.
76. This is also valid even if instead of ἐν οἷς one reads rather ἐν αἷς.
77. Jülicher, *Einleitung*, 148, 183.
78. Spitta, *Zur Geschichte*.

with those people who with Pauline sentences and sayings want to gloss over their moral tepidness, since he explicates in 2 Pet 3:13–18 the same thought and concept in another manner that does not remind us of any of Paul's phrases. But moreover one does not need to believe that with the first passage the writer is taking issue against Paul and that his explanations factually counter Paul's teachings. From his vantage point these explanations could just as well appear to be meant as interpretation and justification for certain dubious statements of Paul that have been misunderstood. One is dealing here—and I am thinking of the very visible proof-text from Jas 2:20–26, born out of the awkwardness and embarrassment of that verse—with nothing other than how one has dealt with the Old Testament when a mean-spirited understanding has usurped very difficult passages. If such a view is at all possible, so it is also very probable. For such a late document as actually the Letter to James is and considering the likelihood that it has come from a Christian pen, it must not at all be demonstrated that Paul is the authority but that he is not just such an authority. One can further add the observation that the letter appears with other passages to make direct use of Paul's letters. Thus he may be specifically named in this interrelationship. Naturally, we would then have yet another special Paul, "the Paul of *Sola fide*," but not one who projected Luther's understanding of Paul.

CHAPTER III

LITERARY FORM AND COMPOSITION

If the Second Letter to the Thessalonians is to be understood as a pseudepigraphon, then it is not enough to discuss and debate the circumstances of its origin. Its form must also be closely scrutinized. Yet here we will take only a fleeting look at the style and mode of expression of this document.

In any event, we are only very imperfectly familiar with Paul's language. Thus one is not able to gain and assess anything definite and uncontested from the unique linguistic features that we encounter here. On the other hand, one should not be able to find any positive characteristic of authenticity in the apparent Pauline style and mode of expression. Jülicher's view[1] is that one must marvel at the forger who has so skillfully copied the Pauline style.

I do not agree with this. Since a good part of the plagiarism has been taken from the first letter, one first has to first collect the borrowings and forged material in a definite copy. Once that is accomplished, then the specific Pauline material itself is substantially reduced. What remains after that contains enough expressions and evidence that make the impression of Pauline origin and character uncertain, and at first impression directly appears to thwart them.[2] I seriously doubt that anyone will be able to better

---

1. Jülicher, *Einleitung*, 47.
2. Bornemann, *Die Thessalonicherbriefe*, 462. He finds evidence for a very strong, Old Testament coloring and quality of the language.

demonstrate more definite aspects of Pauline style in both of the independent sections of the letter—2 Thess 1:5–10; 2:1–12—than in the First Letter of Peter.

If for other reasons the inauthenticity of the letter might be asserted, no one will thus be able to arrive at the conclusion that someone other than Paul speaks here, even when at least a considerable part of the linguistic characteristics have been derived from this material.

It is certainly no coincidence that the writer writes κύριος where Paul always tends to use θεός. For it is most certainly possible that God and not Christ has been meant with the appellation of κύριος in 2 Thess 3:16 because the original text of 1 Thess 5:23 even speaks of God (ὁ θεὸς τῆς εἰρήνης). Then too from the verses of 2 Thess 2:13; 3:3; cf. 3:5 one will likewise arrive at the same conclusion when one compares the parallels 1 Thess 1:4 (ἀδελφοὶ ἠγαπημένοι ὑπὸ τοῦ θεοῦ) and 1 Thess 5:24 (πιστὸς ὁ καλῶν). Considering the content of these statements it is very improbable the writer used Christ for God in these verses. Similarly with many contemporary Christians it was really much more common for him to say "the Lord" with many phrases.[3] In conclusion, it would be much the same if one preferred the view that the writer understood and loved to translate the statements that Paul made about God as a reference to Christ.

Also the twofold expression εὐχαριστεῖν ὀφείλομεν from 2 Thess 1:3; 2:13 rather than the εὐχαριστοῦμεν of 1 Thess 1:2; 2:13 is hardly a coincidence.[4] The rewriting of ὀφείλομεν (ὀφείλετε etc.) is used very often in the Letter to Barnabas.[5] Cf. Bar 1:7; 2:1, 10; 4:6; 6:18; 7:11; 13:3; see also I Clem 40:1. In the light of these parallels one will not want to make too much of the expression, εὐχαριστεῖν ὀφείλομεν, and thus from the "Feeling of Responsibility" that Paul should have here for emphatic reasons. Should

---

3. Holtzmann, "Zum zweiten Thessalonicherbrief," 101–2; Spitta, *Zur Geschichte*, 128; Zahn, *Einleitung*, 182. According to Zahn "it is clear that a forger would not have replaced one of Paul's commonly used expressions such as 'God of Peace' with such an unheard of title as 'the Lord of Peace.'" Is not everything so obvious! As if with our writer a thorough familiarity with our critical choice of words were to be presumed!

4. Holtzmann, "Zum zweiten Thessalonicherbrief," 98; Zahn, *Einleitung*, 175. Zahn considers it not believable that a forger "could have placed such an unheard of sentence in the mouth of Paul, and not once but twice in the authentic and inauthentic letters of Paul: 'we are obligated to thank God for you at all times.'" Then too from the interwoven time periods reflected with 2 Thess 1:10–12 and 2 Thess 2:3–9 that others find so suspicious, Zahn knows how to forge the "Mark of Authenticity." See Holtzmann for all the periods of 2 Thess 1:3–12.

5. Rauch, Untitled Entry, *Zeitschrift*, 458.

these expressions have been especially familiar to the writer precisely as a kind of formula of the liturgical language? With the mere intent to "elevate" the argument I can see no real reason for the choice of the expression. The ὀφείλομεν is also found with εὐχαριστεῖν (ὑπερευχαριστεῖν, εὐχαριστοῦντες αἰνεῖν) in I Clem 38:4 and Bar 5:3;7:1.

Moreover with the use of κλῆσις in 2 Thess 1:11 that is certainly to be understood as an imminent call and that in this sense has no other equivalent in Paul's letters, and with εἵλατο of 2 Thess 2:13 instead of ἐξελέξατο, and several other expressions a trace of non-Pauline usage can be documented with greater or less probability. Biblical criticism has assuredly gone much too far with such assessments and opinions since it has often overrated the significance of the linguistic arguments.

Yet it is not my intent to take much time for these matters that have been dealt with many times. It is enough to conclude that the language of this letter gives evidence of a great similarity to Pauline usage that is known to us. At the same time, there is much departure from that usage as it is appropriate and suitable for a writer who so very closely follows a Pauline original but was also familiar with more than one Pauline letter.

The entire atmosphere of the letter does not to any less degree justify or verify the assumption of its inauthenticity, for it actually gives definite support for such a view. How much less fresh and direct, how much drier, official, and impersonal is its tone in comparison with that of the first letter, as for example both Spitta and Bornemann have so very well described.[6] This stance is most appropriate for an imitator.

We understand this even better when we remember an earlier observation.[7] That element of the personable, individual, and cordial warmth of the first letter that so readily marks it as an original, non-contrived[8] literary

---

6. Bornemann, *Die Thessalonicherbriefe*, 465ff.; Spitta, *Zur Geschichte*, 116ff.; Cf. Zahn, *Einleitung*, 174. Bornemann wants to explain from the apects and character of the impersonable, neutral etc. that Paul out of a sense of pedagogical wisdom has omitted names and all other people from the text of his letters to protect them (467, 481). That is nonetheless a contrived and subjective disposition of the matter.

7. See 33 above.

8. The judgment and assessment of the Tübingen School continues to exercise a consequential influence over the Pauline letters forasmuch as the authenticity of the four primary letters tends to appear one level more certain that that of the First Letter to the Thessalonians or the Letter to the Philippians. I do not doubt the authenticity of the Letter to the Romans. But if I were to assess the various, different levels, so then my doubt about this letter would be always more understandable than with regard to the two other letters.

composition lies for the most part in its second and third chapters ending with 1 Thess 3:10. We have already seen that the writer has completely skipped over these sections. Then too of course all of the realistic characteristics of the actual communal situation have been omitted that the first letter recorded.

Irrespective of this a perceptible difference lies behind the commanding tone and character of certain sentences that the first letter does not give any evidence of. The passage of 2 Thess 3:6–15 is especially important here.[9]

> "But we command you, brothers, in the name of our Lord Jesus Christ, to withdraw yourselves from every brother who walks slovenly and not according to the instruction (παράδοσις) that they have received from us."[10] (2 Thess 3:6)

> "Whenever one of you does not obey my written word, mark this one out so that you do not associate with him . . . " (2 Thess 3:14)

An explanation for this can be easily given. Hopefully everyone will discover here with regard to this matter that the pseudo-apostle is of the opinion that he should take up an apostolic tone, whereas the real apostle does not.

Several comments have been made concerning the actual literary technique of the writer. We have to expand on these, as we peruse through the entire letter from this point of view.

First of all, the writer copied the address of the first letter word by word. By all means it is clear that he joined the words ἐν θεῷ πατρὶ ἡμῶν καὶ κυρίῳ Ἰησοῦ Χριστῷ with the preceding, since otherwise he would not have been able to add and place ἀπὸ θεοῦ πατρὸς κτλ with the χάρις ὑμῖν καὶ εἰρήνη.[11] Whether or not he has really arrived at the meaning that Paul intended is rather doubtful. Despite the obvious placement of words, the analogy of the other Pauline addresses—in which χάρις ὑμῖν καὶ εἰρήνη never occurs without an addition (ἀπὸ θεοῦ πατρὸς κτλ)—suggests that the words ἐν θεῷ κτλ are to be combined with χάρις ὑμῖν καὶ εἰρήνη. However that might be, we most certainly recognize the strange and thoughtless addition of the

---

9. Cf. Spitta, *Zur Geschichte*, 117–18. He refers to 2 Thess 2:15; 3:4 among other verses.

10. Παρελάβοσαν. The LA [Western reading] παρελάβετε is the correction.

11. When the redactors as a rule strongly punctuate the text before χάρις in 1 Thess 1:1 (see 4 above), so then they will have been guided by the analogy of 2 Thess 1:1–2. But this is not conclusive (also opposed to Bornemann for 1 Thess 1:1).

second phrase of ἀπὸ θεοῦ πατρὸς κτλ as that of a copyist. He expanded the stark and bare χάρις ὑμῖν καὶ εἰρήνη with this phrase because they lingered still in his ear from the headings of Paul's other letters.

The writer freely copied the heading of his letter from that of the first letter. But then after the mention of διωγμοί and θλίψεις (2 Thess 1:4), he proceeds with a small digression of 2 Thess 1:5–12 his own way and gives expression to his own sentiment. That has been previously discussed.[12] Here verses 11 and 12 refer once more back to the characteristic statements of greeting at the beginning. One can well and clearly imagine the train of thought. The actual digression has been ended. The writer knows now that at the beginning he spoke of thanksgiving but that he did mention and speak of petition and prayer for his readers that the first letter presented. So he proceeds to make that up, whereby at the same time he admittedly continues the last train of thought. It appears to me that when at this point the very peculiar expression ἔργον πίστεως[13] arises that stands at the beginning of the thanksgiving in the first letter, so that provides a definite verification for the use of the first letter.

After this introduction, which itself contains eschatological elements, the very extensive eschatological passage immediately follows. That is assuredly not coincidence, even so much less than that the first letter's corresponding eschatological discourse is found at the end of that letter. Obviously the writer hurries immediately on to this topic because already at this point he wants to give expression to the matter that lies close to his heart. Thus we understand why the entire parallel structure of the two letters has been interrupted at this juncture.

The real concern of the writer has been expressed with the passage 2 Thess 2:1–12. Now he returns once more to the original. If one keeps in view that he could not begin any further elaboration of the historical and personal content of 1 Thess 2:1—3:10 and therefore has omitted it, it will thus not be difficult to understand the progressive continuation of the letter.

After the eschatological discourse his view remained fixed at first on the resumption of the thanksgiving passage of 1 Thess 2:13, particularly with the oblique ἡμεῖς[14] but very probably also by means of the relatedness of 2 Thess 2:14 with 1 Thess 2:12. At the same time thereby his eye returns to the thanksgiving theme of the first chapter. That is demonstrated by the

---

12. See 17 and 51 above.
13. Kern, "Über 2 Thess 2:1–12," 212. Cf. his comment.
14. See 20 above.

Literary Form and Composition

ἀδελφοὶ ἠγαπημένοι ὑπὸ τοῦ θεοῦ and the ὅτι εἵλατο ὑμᾶς ὁ θεός (cf. 1 Thess 1:4). Then he hurries on past the personal comments of Paul of chapters 2 and 3—the στήκετε in 2 Thess 2:15 thereby appears to him to have remained in the sense taken from 1 Thess 3:8. But then with 1 Thess 3:11–13 he encounters a general wish that he is able to appropriately make use of with his own version, 2 Thess 2:16–17.

Thus when the request for the intercession of the readers follows that, introduced by τὸ λοιπόν (1 Thess 4:1: λοιπόν), it already sounds in and of itself just like a closing verse. This impression is further reinforced for the προσεύχεσθε, ἀδελφοί, and περὶ ἡμῶν appear to have been taken from the closing of the first letter and also since the πιστὸς δέ ἐστιν ὁ κύριος (2 Thess 3:3) point to him (1 Thess 5:24). Additionally it may also be added that the train of thought in 2 Thess 3:1–5 or actually beginning already with 2 Thess 2:13 becomes peculiarly erratic, agitated, and disquieting. With almost every sentence there is a new theme: 2 Thess 2:13–14 presents a thanksgiving, 2 Thess 2:15 an admonition, 2 Thess 2:16–17 a prayer-wish, 2 Thess 3:1 a request for an intercession for the Gospel and the Apostle, 2 Thess 3:3 an expression of reliance on God abruptly added on, 2 Thess 3:4 another expression of trust that refers to the behavior and conduct of the readers, and 2 Thess 3:5 once more another prayer-wish. This last sentence is almost a duplicate of 2 Thess 2:16–17 and has been taken from 1 Thess 3:11. This original verse has once more been exploited, whereby the κατευθῦναι admittedly must lose its relationship to Paul's travel plans (1 Thess 3:11 κατευθῦναι τὴν ὁδὸν ἡμῶν πρὸς ὑμᾶς) and become a rather drab and colorless expression (κατευθῦναι ὑμῶν τὰς καρδίας . . .). It is hardly mere subjective sentiment when I express the view that the writer here in this section no longer knows how to proceed and that his copious dependence on the original results not without a definite correlation to the ebbing of the flow of thought. According to this observation we will assume that originally he wanted to close the letter with 2 Thess 3:1 or rather with 2 Thess 2:16–17.[15] That in itself is evidence that after the completion of the eschatological discourse it became clear to him that the real purpose that motivated him to take up the pen had already been carried to its end.

Irrespective of the interpretation that for the readers the word of God is vibrant and resonates among them (καθὼς καὶ πρὸς ὑμᾶς), a fact that could be well explained from the previously used short verse of 1 Thess 2:1, which testifies that the Thessalonians have properly received the word of

---

15. Holtzmann, *Einleitung*, 212–13; von Hoffmann, *Die heilige Schrift*.

God, the content of the solicited intercession of 2 Thess 3:1, 2 has no equivalent in the original letter. That is remarkable because of the second half of the verse: ἵνα ῥυσθῶμεν ἀπὸ τῶν ἀτόπων καὶ πονηρῶν ἀνθρώπων. At first this sounds like a reference to specific persons and events. Precisely because the first letter does not provide a proper explanation, it appears unusual and strange for a Pseudo-Paul and even more appropriate for the Apostle who at least with this remark would be referring to something about the contemporary situation in Corinth. Therefore some have willingly found here evidence for an allusion to the reports of Acts 18:12–17.

Nonetheless this expression is not at all specific or typical, for it appears that the writer is making use of a biblical mode of expression. Isa 25:4 taken from the LXX states: ἀπὸ πονηρῶν ἀνθρώπων ῥύσῃ αὐτούς.[16] If the form of this verse is to be thus understood, then it appears that the thought would be as it emerges from very simple deliberation that the writer is aware that Paul as an Evangelist and Apostle stood over and against a world that for the most part did not believe his message and even demonstrated enmity toward him. The statement, οὐ γὰρ πάντων ἡ πίστις, leads to this general understanding. If we further assume that the writer has already sharply spoken out two times against such ἄτοποι and πονηροὶ ἄνθρωποι (2 Thess 1:6–10; 2:10–12) who are the oppressors of the believers and the despisers of the truth, so one will not take offence when he names and specifies the Apostle along with the "Propagation of the Word" as the actual content for the intercession which he requests. There is no real reason to consider specific people and definite events. The προσεύχεσθε, ἀδελφοί, περὶ ἡμῶν occurs in the first letter without any further description.

Here the writer abandons the initial thought of ending the letter. With 2 Thess 3:6–15 he follows with another discourse of admonition where the unity, flow of thought, and liveliness of the composition is distinctly contrasted to the preceding. It is very likely that at this point his earlier comments appear too brief for him. Above all, we will assume that the words of the first letter about quiescence and work subsequently come into view, demand his attention, and appear especially important and appropriate for his audience.

As a manner of explanation he remembered that Paul had spoken about work with a second passage found in 1 Thess 2:9. He welcomed Paul's view about work because it afforded him the opportunity to present his

---

16 Bornemann, *Die Thessalonicherbriefe*, 388, 533. He has made a remark about this. Cf. Rom 15:31; *Did* 5:2.

word of warning and admonition. Although for the most part he could simply copy these words of Paul, admittedly he must modify the Pauline train of thought in this relational context. It is clear that Paul had not deliberately intended to provide the Thessalonians with an exemplary paradigm for work with his manual work.[17] Biblical scholars have often enough taken exception[18] to this comment of the second letter. Yet without further engaging the discussion of this question we may conclude in this matter that biblical criticism has well understood the extent to which Paul himself could consider his work from this aspect and standpoint.

It is worth mentioning that the earlier letter does not speak at all about a precept or code of work. So far as the Pauline παράδοσις is referred to, the text reminds us only of the personal example of the Apostle (2 Thess 3:7–9) and his verbal direction (2 Thess 3:10)—both points that the first letter readily and distinctly presented. One could be tempted[19] namely to relate the sentence about ἐπιστολή from 2 Thess 3:14 to this letter because the copied, original verse of 1 Thess 4:11 immediately precedes 2 Thess 3:12. Yet this original verse itself occurs as a present, not an earlier request or demand, and the text makes no mention at all about an earlier demand as such. Therefore it is much more likely that διὰ τῆς ἐπιστολῆς is to be understood from the viewpoint of the second letter. The obedience of which 2 Thess 3:14 speaks is naturally intended and aimed at the definite command (παραγγέλλομεν 2 Thess 3:12). Also 2 Thess 3:11 (ἀκούομεν γάρ τινας περιπατοῦντας ἐν ὑμῖν ἀτάκτως) is not to be read as a report about the disheveled transformation of Christians whom the Apostle came to visit. The writer proceeds here simply as a forger and composes, to a certain extent, from the viewpoint of the first letter but not with verbatim retrospection to it. He could have done this and refer thus to the previous text of the original just as 2 Thess 2:15 gives us an example. Much less easily to the contrary could Paul ignore the fact that he had already once with a letter admonished the community about their work.

From the first letter it can be concluded that the instruction about work does not merely refer to the idle ones themselves (1 Thess 5:12) but also to the conduct of the others to them (1 Thess 5:6, 13–16).

17. Cf. 2 Thess 3:9: ἵνα ἑαυτοὺς τύπον δῶμεν ὑμῖν. The preceeding words, οὐχ ὅτι οὐκ ἔχομεν, remind one of a Pauline explanation and expression such as 1 Cor 9:4ff.

18. Cf. Hilgenfeld, *Einleitung*, 644.

19. Zahn, *Einleitung*, 165, 173. See especially 173. His proposal that the mention of ἐάν in the second letter could be presumed to be a conditional conjunction does not convince us.

The Authenticity of the Second Letter to the Thessalonians

After the completion of this explanation the writer of our letter (2 Thess 3:16) returns to the conclusion of the original letter (1 Thess 5:23). The admonitions that precede the closing remarks have been disregarded. Nevertheless one can easily see that the beginning of this passage (1 Thess 5:13 (?), 14) has already influenced the discussion about work (2 Thess 3:15). The transition from 1 Thess 4:11 to 1 Thess 5:14 and then on to 1 Thess 5:23 demonstrates here how the eye of the writer has proceeded through the text. Then when the abrasive tone of 2 Thess 3:14 is rather noticeablyl replaced with the milder expression of 2 Thess 3:15 (καὶ μὴ ὡς ἐχθρὸν ἡγεῖσθε, κτλ), so this exchange that is almost tantamount to a complete paradox explains best of all here that the writer was prompted by the original text itself (1 Thess 5:14, cf. 13) to modify the original verses.[20]

Very possibly the special reference to his own letter (2 Thess 3:14) has been elicited with regard to the relationship to 1 Thess 5:27. Both verses coincide with one another since they demand serious attention to the written letter. For that matter one will find the τῷ λόγῳ ἡμῶν διὰ τῆς ἐπιστολῆς (2 Thess 3:14) very naturally characteristic of the Pseudo-Paul. He distinctly emphasizes the letter because he knows it is a matter of authority that he claims for himself. From Paul's point of view the addendum διὰ τῆς ἐπιστολῆς as viewed from the standpoint of the second letter would in my opinion have been unmotivated and superfluous.[21] The mention of ἐπιστολῆς in 1 Thess 5:27 is an entirely different matter, for here one is dealing with an oral reading of the letter.

The concluding wish of 2 Thess 3:16 is much shorter than that of 1 Thess 5:23. The phrase ἐν παντὶ τρόπῳ could well be a summary of many destinations that are alluded to with this verse.

Additionally another matter arises in this regard which especially the very proficient study of K. Dick[22] has recently called attention to. It is well-known that with the first letter Paul always uses the first person plural to refer to himself with the exception of verses 1 Thess 2:18; 3:5; 5:27. The interpretation of this observation does not concern us here. We ask only how the second letter responds to this usage. The writer of the second letter likewise also uses the first person plural, and only in verses 2 Thess 2:5 and 2 Thess 3:17 does the singular occur. This second verse disqualifies

---

20. Holtzmann, Untitled Entry, *Schenkels Bibellexikon*, 508; Holtzmann, "Zum zwetien Thessaloniherbrief," 102–3.

21. Zahn, *Einleitung*, 173. He has obviously perceived this.

22. Dick, *Der schriftstellerische Plural*, 73–74. See especially 73.

itself from any consideration because its structure allows only the use of the singular. It could perhaps well appear to be a striking coincidence that the writer shows the same fondness for the literary plural or—according to the other concept and version of the questionable occurrence—for the constant consideration of the other "co-writers" (Silvanus and Timothy) as Paul himself does in his authentic letters. Yet neither a special interest for the helpers of Paul nor the same stylistic tendency on the part of our writer can be assumed. On the other hand it is rather artificial to attribute to him an intentional replication of such a small matter, that author who hardly had the eyes to see it and who has demonstrated much freedom over and against the words of Paul. But by itself the dependence on the original does not have to have been intentional. Therefore the proposal of an involuntary and unintentional plagiarism can well be documented here. A comparison teaches that the "we" has actually been used in all of the primary verses and passages of the first letter. Thus it is only natural that the plural was retained even where there were no distinct parallels. The exception of 2 Thess 2:5 could best be explained by the observation that in this section the original did not play a role. Nonetheless nothing of this can be definitely proved or demonstrated. But it is certain that the writer would not have thought, as Dick assumes in his concept of the inauthenticity of the letter, to copy the singular or plural (*numerus*) from the first letter.

The previous comments demonstrate that the assumption of the inauthenticity of the letter is not at all a false key both for the understanding of its entire composition as well as for many of its particular characteristics. Now the question arises as to what extent the writer has pursued the original text. Has he established for himself in a rather naïve, unintentional, and convenient dependence on the framework for that which he really wants to validate and bring to fruition? Or did he have a definite awareness of the fact that the similarity of the original text would suggest the content of his letter?

One would like to suppose that a certain purpose played a role here, especially when with the closing he seeks to defend his letter with a special explanation about the possibility of a mistrustful reception of it. Far removed from what one would fear with a literary imitation, he may have if anything felt himself secured with the original. But certainly considering all of the details one cannot conceive of the complete use and imitation of Paul's letter as the result of reflection and intended style. Thus the dependence must have been at many points much more exact.

With my analysis of the letter I am rather certain that I have not repudiated this view and have imputed to the writer a fictitious technique and procedure. Yet from another point of view one may well raise an objection against the conception of the entire literary project that we have presupposed. Grimm has already given voice to this matter.[23] He has taken issue with Baur and asks if for every appropriate verse or passage of the second letter one is required to find several putative or actual parallels in order to substantiate copied or duplicated material taken from the first letter. With such an endeavor a whimsical manner of literary activity would be ascribed to the Pseudo-Paul, since in order to form only one sentence, he would have looked around to two or three verses of the original and out of those would have combined words and thoughts for his sentence.

On the one hand, this objection is not the worst proposal since it compels one to conceive of the literary activity of a falsifier as a concrete process. However, the point of his argument has been dethroned and eliminated if the earlier expressed observation[24] is really correct that for the most part the majority of the similarities distinctly relate and combine one single verse or passage of the one with just such a one from the other letter. If on the other hand as opposed to that many parallels from several related verses of the first letter actually coincide, support, and explain a verse of the second letter, that is not at all an incomprehensible occurrence. Several examples have already demonstrated this. There was nothing irrational about the fact that alongside 2 Thess 2:13 and 1 Thess 2:18, the verse from 1 Thess 1:4 is also reminiscent of them. Additionally, 2 Thess 3:8, which occurs in the middle of a passage, reminds one of 1 Thess 4:11–12 and demonstrates a clear and special dependence on 1 Thess 2:9. Other such cases can be similarly explained. It is most natural that single phrases and verses anchor themselves in one's memory with the reading of the opened letter and that they might well penetrate the text where other verses are primarily authoritative and decisive. On the other hand, if someone *during the process of writing* used an original text and easily skimmed over large sections of it, that person would have combined material that did not relate. No one can accurately assess everything in such cases, and no one can demand that one be able to accomplish such.

Irregularities and ambiguities often result in dependent writings when they have been derived from a slavish dependence on the original

---

23. Grimm, "Die Echtheit," *Studien*, 801.

24. See 18ff. above.

text—yet not always. We have already encountered a few such cases with our research. The non-analogous ἡμεῖς (δὲ) of 2 Thess 2:13 explains the unusual addition of ἀπὸ θεοῦ πατρὸς ἡμῶν κτλ in the greeting, and finally the peculiar and specific relationship of 2 Thess 3:15 to 2 Thess 3:14 is to be singled out and remembered here.[25] Further examples of this kind have often been found. At least with two cases the judgment of critical scholars seems to be very probable.

The usage of πλεονάζει ἡ ἀγάπη ἑνὸς ἑκάστου πάντων ὑμῶν εἰς ἀλλήλους of 2 Thess 1:3 is incorrect to the extent that εἰς ἀλλήλους is related to a singular form. After ἑνὸς ἑκάστου one would expect to find ὑμῶν rather than πάντων ὑμῶν. Πάντων can easily be derived from 1 Thess 1:2. But the combination of the singular with εἰς ἀλλήλους might be easily explained from the influence of the verse 1 Thess 3:12: ὑμᾶς ὁ κύριος πλεονάσαι (here it is transitive) . . . τῇ ἀγάπῃ εἰς ἀλλήλους.[26] But the matter is really not obvious.

The second case deals with these words that immediately follow the brief thanksgiving: ὥστε αὐτοὺς ἡμᾶς ἐν ὑμῖν ἐγκαυχᾶσθαι (2 Thess 1:4). Here that αὐτοὺς ἡμᾶς distinctively presupposes an opposite. The exegetes acknowledge this for the most part but find themselves faced with a dilemma because no striking opposite can be derived from the context itself. Nevertheless an explanation for the dilemma results when one finds the opposite in the *object* of the pride and praise because the writers do not merely praise the Thessalonians but even themselves for their own sakes.[27] It is very likely possible that αὐτοὺς ἡμᾶς is to be considered simply as an expression of the apostolic dignity and that the discreet thoughts or words are to be accepted for what is expressed. Thus they would explain the matter as follows: when we ourselves praise someone, so that means more than when others do that. It is still more likely to find a relationship in these words to 1 Thess 1:7–8 to the others who proclaim there the praise of the Thessalonians. Thus the αὐτοὺς ἡμᾶς appears assuredly to have been expressed with a very special exaltation.[28]

---

25. See 79 above.

26. Holtzmann, "Zum zweiten Thessalonicherbrief," 100; Schmiedel, Untitled Entry, *Handkommentar*. But Schmiedel just as also Holtzmann would like to derive the ἑνὸς ἑκάστου from 1 Thess. 2:11.

27. Bornemann, *Die Thessalonicherbriefe*. (According to A. Buttmann and Laurent).

28. Hilgenfeld, Untitled Entry, *Zeitschrift*, 243; Holtzmann, "Zum zweiten Thessalonicherbrief," 100; Schmiedel, Untitled Entry, *Handkommentar*, z St., 9–11. Cf. also 1 Thess 1:1b, 9 and the opposition: ἡμᾶς—αὐτοί.

The extent to which other particular words and expressions that present themselves without any difficulty and which receive a special light[29] of emphasis by means of a comparison with the first letter are not to be considered and examined here.

---

29. Holtzmann, "Zum zweiten Thessalonicherbrief," 99. For example an expression such as 2 Thess 1:3: ὑπεραυξάνει ἡ πίστις ὑμῶν.

CHAPTER IV

THE LETTER AS FORGERY

If the Second Letter to the Thessalonians does not come from the hand of Paul then it is a forgery, a falsified document. The warning of scholars of modern biblical criticism is certainly justified to the extent that pseudonymous literary activity of the early Christian period is not to be judged by the moral precepts of our day. Yet all too often it sounds as if the concept of literary plagiarism did not even exist. On the contrary, one cannot believe that.

Certainly whoever makes the effort to clearly distinguish conceptually between "harmless pseudonymity" and "forgery" or "falsification" will find that the boundary between the two cannot easily be drawn. By no means can an attempt to clarify these matters be parenthetically made here. I assert only the following: when one is able to speak at all about falsification, then this activity and rubric is not in our case to be presented and circulated as Baur and Weizsäcker have used them.

One will at first thereby consider that the writer has deliberately carried out a fiction (the composition of a fictional letter) that extends to the solemn, ceremonial confirmation of the authenticity of the letter (2 Thess 3:17). Yet it is perhaps more important that this document has been written for a very concrete purpose which is to prove that certain opponents are most assuredly wrong about a definite question. It is this matter that brings the development of the fiction fully to light. Such a document would not at all be true to itself without the intent to deceive, and this intent and purpose cannot be separated from an awareness of the untruthfulness of the allegations.

Precisely because one is dealing here with just such a concrete purpose and aim, it is not sufficient to cite for an explication[1] the following convention: "to write in the name of some one prominent or a greater person." This convention can have accommodated the literary intent of the writer, but it cannot be the decisive matter here. It is also not "a" greater person in whose name a general, optional teaching or admonition has been proclaimed and delivered. It is rather much more that most definite person Paul whose opinion has been called into question.

From a moral point of view there is little expressed with the classification of forgery. We cannot know what this course of action might have meant conventionally for the falsifier himself because we simply do not know him. We will nonetheless judge and evaluate him very differently from a Christian who in our day might have done something similar. It can hardly be denied that at that time one was less sensitive and actually extremely less sensitive than today about a violation of the truth *once it dealt with a religious purpose*. Our writer pursued a religious purpose from his viewpoint. He placed the "truth" as a matter of the correct teaching over and against an alarming and dubious opinion about the End Time. Furthermore, we will credit him with the understanding that he has verified the actual and truest opinion of Paul and that he did not sense a sacrilege against Paul.

Moreover when the untruthfulness that he afforded himself is judged from a hyperbolized and exaggerated point of view, nothing may be proved or determined against the probability of the assumption itself. For no one can verify that this man, who for us is simply a Mr. X, has committed a forgery or not; for we cannot determine if he is to be trusted. Nonetheless when some speak to the defenders of the authenticity of this letter as if one needs to compel and urge them to accept the corollary that it is a brazen forgery only for the purpose of demonstrating that they are wrong, so that has resulted from the fact that one assesses the literary works of the New Testament with another measure other than that used for works of ancient church literature. Why, for example, did no one make the self-assertions of the Gospel of Peter the basis of the real evidence of its authenticity when that fragment was discovered and came to light? Some reasons could well have been found. An

---

1. Schmiedel, Untitled Entry, *Handkommentar*, 10–12.

The Letter as Forgery

actual difficulty might exist in our case only when there was no credible motif for its composition. But that is not so, as we have already seen.

The closing remark of 2 Thess 3:17 must be once more referred to and considered. It contains nothing whatsoever that contradicts our viewpoint, for it only favors it.

Biblical criticism has asked how it was that Paul comes to assert and affirm in such an early letter that the autographic greeting in his own hand is his "mark" in every letter. How might he place there the verification of the authentication of this letter as the purpose of these autographic closing remarks when namely 1 Cor 16:21 has absolutely no such meaning? Finally how has it come about that many of the extant later letters of Paul (The Second Letter to the Corinthians, Romans, and Philippians) mention nothing at all about such an autographic greeting? These questions should not be pursued anew here. Yet no one can deny that if 2 Thess 3:17 is to be understood as one of Paul's comments, it presupposes after all something most remarkable.[2] On the other hand, it can be said that the impression of such suspicious deliberateness with such a comment may well lead one astray. First Thessalonians 5:27 states: ἐνορκίζω ὑμᾶς τὸν κύριον ἀναγνωσθῆναι τὴν ἐπιστολὴν πᾶσιν τοῖς ἀδελφοῖς. If these words occurred in the second letter, one would most probably find them also to be suspicious.[3]

Meanwhile, however, it is thus an entirely different matter for us if we do not understand 2 Thess 2:2 as an allusion to an actual or putative forged letter. With regard to such a presupposition—and this prerequisite is necessary—the ὅ ἐστιν σημεῖον ἐν πάσῃ ἐπιστολῇ, viewed as Paul's affirmation, becomes immediately mysterious because no definite purpose or cause for it can be found. As a matter of fact it becomes "the betrayer."[4]

Now certainly just these very words should not be suitable for a forger. For all of the extant letters of Paul would then not have such a closing. But if when such an allegation does not arise from statistical and historical interests but rather from a definite intent and purpose, would such scrupulous exactness be expected! If this autographic closing stood out in several of Paul's letters, so then one could easily make from this a customary practice of the Apostle Paul and no less easily highlight his intent that he wanted

---

2. Reuss, *Die Geschichte*, 74. He states: "2 Thess 3:17 would be fallacious and deceitful only when other reasons legitimize a doubt about it."

3. Baur, *Paulus*. Baur actually saw in them a characteristic feature for a later composition of the first letter.

4. Baur, *Paulus*, 406; Kern, "Über 2 Thess 2:1–12," 209; Wiezsäcker, *Das Apostolische Zeitalter*, 250, 260.

thereby to make his property distinguishable.⁵ But by no means did the writer of this letter need to examine this practice for all of Paul's letters that were known to him.

In and of itself perhaps this answer is not sufficient. The most obvious element with our view of the matter is not actually that the ὁ ἀσπασμὸς τῇ ἐμῇ χειρὶ Παύλου is not found in all of the letters, but much more rather that it is distinctly omitted in the original text the writer used. Certainly this is to be understood. The writer would not have even thought about the formulation of this thought which he had not taken from the first letter. We may not impute to him the consideration of critical scholars. But who can tell us that he did not also have just such a prerequisite for the other letters that do not speak of the autographic signature? He could have wanted initially to give the greeting not only already with the words ὁ ἀσπασμὸς τῇ ἐμῇ χειρὶ Παύλου themselves, but rather first of all with the following wish of blessing in 2 Thess 3:18 (also possibly 2 Thess 3:16).⁶ But over and against this exegesis of the texts there is nothing that can be objected to. It appears to be true that the closing wishes of Paul's letters generally were understood under the impression of 1 Cor 16:21, Gal 6:11, and Col 4:18 as the autographic greeting of the Apostle's own hand.⁷ If Paul were the writer, then the relationship of the explanation of 2 Thess 3:17 to the closing of the First Letter to the Thessalonians would by no means be clear. At least so long as he says that the autographic greeting of his own hand is to be the sign of the authenticity in every letter; but not, as one would like for it to say,⁸ that *from now on* it should be the mark of the authenticity in every letter sent *to the Thessalonians*. Both remarks indicate and point to the obvious difference: the simple ὅ ἐστιν σημεῖον ἐν πάσῃ ἐπιστολῇ definitively disputes the implied and suggested explanation.

Yet how can the writer allow Paul to write: οὕτως γράφω? Must the readers have not noticed here that the closing word might well be a deception because Paul's handwriting was not even to be seen? Or perhaps the closing has been written with a manipulated handwriting in order to distinguish and set it (the closing) apart from the rest. The most simple

---

5. Cf. 38 above.

6. Baur, *Paulus*, 488–89; Schmiedel, Untitled Entry, *Handkommentar*.

7. Von Hoffmann, *Die heilige Schrift*, 358; Schmiedel, Untitled Entry, *Handkommentar*, 9–46; Weizsäcker, *Das Apostolische Zeitalter*, 195. Biblical criticism has rarely outside of these three letters found autographic closing remarks from Paul's own hand.

8. Klöpper, "Der 2 Brief," 114; Holtzmann, Untitled Entry, *Theologische Literatur*, col 27; Westrik, *De Echtheid*, 57–58.

explanation about how the writer came to the phrase οὕτως γράφω is to be found in Gal 6:11: ἴδετε πηλίκοις ὑμῖν γράμμασιν ἔγραψα τῇ ἐμῇ χειρί.[9] The Letter to the Galatians appears to be known to him on the basis of another verse.[10] But he certainly did not think that there would be any difficulty with his shortened imitation of Gal 6:11. And of course he did not need to. For the forgery of Paul's special handwriting and signature was not a required precondition for the readers' belief in his written document. He read the Letter to the Galatians from a copy that no longer showed and revealed Paul's own handwriting. His own letter could just as well be sent as a copy as if it were the original text.

However, how could the attempt to sign a letter for Paul be successful? Zahn has asked and demanded not without good reason that we submit ourselves to this question in cases that are similar to ours with this letter.[11] I believe that I have successfully honored the correctness of this request, whereby with the above[12] I have demonstrated that the actual address of the (inauthentic) letter for the community of the Thessalonians was from the start not very probable. If the letter originated somewhere very far from Thessalonica, then that question is just as likely not to be definitely answered. But it is a less difficult matter with some other fictional document that really found belief and acceptance in the church. For then no one there was able to monitor the forger, and one was credulous when one was dogmatically satisfied. At the most one can only reflect about how the community of Thessalonica received the letter when it was imported from outside the community as a prestigious document that was already reputable. How much time had elapsed since its composition eludes any definite speculation. If the letter itself had already made its way to Thessalonica in the years

---

9. It is possible that he wrote πηλίκοις = *qualibus*, not = *quantis*. *Qualibus* offers (the meaning or sign for) Itala as from the Vulgate. Chrysostomus z St. (see Tischendorf's Octava) likewise meant that πηλίκοις designated οὐ τὸ μέγεθος, ἀλλὰ τὴν ἀμορφίαν τῶν γραμμάτων. Hesychius explains the following: πηλίκον οἷον, ὁποῖον ποταπόν. Cf. Laurent, Untitled Entry, *Neutestamentliche Studien*, 64.

10. 2 Thess 3:13: ὑμεῖς δέ, ἀδελφοί, μὴ ἐγκακήσητε καλοποιοῦντες; = Gal 6:9: τὸ δὲ καλὸν ποιοῦντες μὴ ἐγκακῶμεν. Perhaps one is also permitted to list Gal 5:10: ἐγὼ πέποιθα εἰς ὑμᾶς ἐν κυρίῳ and 2 Thess 3:4: πεποίθαμεν δὲ ἐν κυρίῳ ἐφ' ὑμᾶς. Other references to which Holtzmann refers on page 106 from his "Zum zweiten Thessalonicherbrief" are not clear to me. By the way Holtzmann throws out the question as to whether or not Gal 6:11 and 2 Thess 3:17 are directly related.

11. Zahn, *Einleitung*, 113–14.

12. See 37–38 above. Cf. 65 above.

between AD 90 and 100, one could easily imagine[13] that perhaps the few living acquaintances of Paul who were young people when the Apostle was in Thessalonica distrusted the authenticity of this letter that was similar to the esteemed and honored first letter. They would have preferred the strength of their memory of that letter, which was unobjectionable with regard to its content and presented no trace of suspicious details. For the time being, however, it is not agreed that the second letter had already been written by the year 100.

A POSSIBLE CHRONOLOGY

The chronological research of the presupposed relationships from the letter itself is not capable of yielding a definite *terminus a quo*. The eschatological position that it espouses cannot be definitely attributed to a specific time. The mention of the words θλίψεις and διωγμοί (2 Thess 1:4) does not by any means lead one with any kind of certainty to the last days of Trajan,[14] even when one relates the words to the time of the writer, i.e., when one does not understand them as taken from the forgery of the first letter. The letter is much too vague, dreary, and colorless. 2 Thess 1:4 does not even afford any difficulties with the view that it is Paul's writing and composition (cf. 1 Thess 2:14–16). A determination of a date by means of the Apocalypse does not come into question if the letter is not dependent upon it, but evidence for this has yet to be provided. The most distinct date is that garnered from the implication that the writer has before him a collection of Paul's letters. I do not venture to say that such a collection is unthinkable before the year AD 100, and not even unimaginable before AD 85 or 90. If, according to all assumptions, the collection is actually very extensive, and when the reputation of the First Letter to the Thessalonians appears to be so definitely rooted that in contrast to the eschatological expectations of the second letter it stands alone as a decisive authority, and when the observations about the outward literary characteristics of Paul's letters such as the postscript have been made, so one will be inclined with regard to our

---

13. Zahn, *Einleitung*, 114, 173. I offer the following remark against Zahn's exaggerated comments. He conceives of and presents the Thessalonians as though they were critical theologians of the twentieth century, especially when he voices the view that 2 Thess 2:2 and 2 Thess 3:17 should have called forth and provoked the "extreme" criticism of the first readers.

14. Hilgenfeld, *Einleitung*, 650.

The Letter as Forgery

knowledge about these matters to postulate a date around AD 85 or 90 or earlier rather than later. But the lack of resounding evidence hardly allows a definite determination of the date to be fixed.

The most reliable date for the *terminus ad quem* is given to us with the fact that Marcion possessed Second Thessalonians and placed it alongside First Thessalonians in his *Apostolikon*. Naturally then this letter must have been written a considerable time before the time of this event. How long or short a time before that is not at all easy to say. Zahn[15] holds the view that it is impossible that one of Paul's ten letters that Marcion had in his collection could have originated during the lifetime of Marcion or after the year 110. This reckoning appears to be debatable. If the second letter is really a forged letter, it can be concluded from the very outset that it was launched and circulated in a circle it was intended to influence; for no one lights a light just to place it under a bushel. If this letter was at all recognized by authoritative circles at the place of its origination, and this we must assume, even the shortest time was sufficient to provide for the development of a reputation for it that the other of Paul's letters were able to attain only after a much longer time. This entire process and its story readily brought about its acceptance. Then everywhere the letter was sent to from the place where it was written, it was similarly accepted. Thus it is then not credible that at the beginning of the second century one would have found the appearance of a new letter of Paul's in itself to be suspicious. So it should not astonish us at all that this letter which for example might have originated in Phrygia may have been placed some five years later in a community of a neighboring province together in a row alongside the other of Paul's known letters. The further distribution to many other provinces must naturally have required much more time. It could quickly have wandered and found its way to Rome where Marcion was a member of the Christian community even before he left and went on his own journey, for those days many canals led to the city. Accordingly it could have come into existence around AD 120 to 125 or even AD 130. Then approximately from about AD 140 to 150 it would have been added and belonged to Marcion's *Apostolikon*. The opinion that its text might have been forged and copied was then truly not known to Marcion. But Marcion's appraisal of the letter does not lead to a precise date for it.

What one could offer and mention about other ancient witnesses for the letter is for the most part insignificant. By no means would Justin give

---

15. Zahn, *Einleitung*, 112.

The Authenticity of the Second Letter to the Thessalonians

any better evidence than Marcion. But the parallels to 2 Thess 2:3–12 that one finds[16] in his writings in no way make a literary use of the letter certain,[17] once one ceases to see in the passage about the Anti-Christ only individual thoughts and musings of the writer. It is precisely so with the similarities to the same passage that one finds in Barnabus and the *Didache*.[18] The phrase, εἴ τις οὐ θέλει ἐργάζεσθαι μηδὲ ἐσθιέτω, from 2 Thess 3:10 looks simply like a proverbial expression. To be sure, it cannot be denied that *Did* 12:8 (ἐργαζέτω καὶ φαγέτω) refers back to this verse, but it does not prove anything.[19] Ignatius truly does not need to have read 2 Thess 2:3: μή τις ὑμᾶς ἐξαπατήσῃ κατὰ μηδένα τρόπον in order to have written Ign. *Eph.* 8:1: μή τις ὑμᾶς ἐξαπατάτω; and the ὀφείλομεν κατὰ πάντα εὐχαριστεῖν αὐτῶν of *1 Clem.* 38:4 along with the similar phrases taken from Bar 5:3; 7:1[20] do not deserve any mention at all. Only one document remains for serious and significant consideration and that is the Letter of Polycarp.

The parallel that is found to be suitable is taken from chapter 11 of the letter of Polycarp to the Philippians.

Poly 11:4: (*Sobrii ergo estote et vos in hoc;*) *et non sicut inimicos tales existimetis, sed* (*sicut passibilia membra et errantia eos revocate*) and 2 Thess 3:15: καὶ μὴ ὡς ἐχθρὸν ἡγεῖσθε, ἀλλὰ (νουθετεῖτε ὡς ἀδελφόν).

The expression ὡς—or perhaps ὥσπερ—ἐχθρὸν ἡγεῖσθαι that would have occurred in the Greek text of the Letter of Polycarp is in and of itself not especially characteristic. Moreover ὥσπερ ἐχθρὸν ἡγεῖσθαι is already to be found in LXX Job 19:11 (cf. 13:24a; 33:10: ὥσπερ ὑπεναντίον ἡγεῖσθαι). Additionally one should not consider the combination of ὡς and ἡγεῖσθαι an unusual occurrence.[21] The similarity of the two verses becomes first of all rather obvious because the exact agreement has come about just in this form. The same combination with καὶ is certainly insignificant and coincidental.[22] But since that with the identical phrase both verses also agree with one another by way of a negative imperative with a following ἀλλά, it

---

16. Cf. Justin Martyr, *Dialogue* 32, 110, (116).

17. Bornemann, *Die Thessalonicherbriefe*, 320. This is against his assessment.

18. Cf. Bar 4:9; 15:5; 18:2. Cf. *Did* 16:3–6.

19. 2 Thess 3:10 has been cited and quoted yet not exactly. See Pseudoignatius, *Ad Magn*, c. 9.

20. See 72 above.

21. Blass, *Neutestamentliche Grammatik*, 91, 241–42, 265; Bornemann, *Die Thessalonicherbriefe*, 398. Cf. Hermas Vis. I 1:7; 2 *Clem* 5:6; Sir 29:4 (ὡς with νομίζειν).

22. It would perhaps be another matter if the opposite relationship of dependence were in question here, because the καὶ after 2 Thess 3:14 certainly attracts one's attention.

is rather certain that this shows with great probability that it has been taken from 2 Thess 3:15, and all the more so because Polycarp sometimes makes use of foreign words.

A second verse from the Letter of Polycarp can be confirmed. Poly 11:3 reports the following: *ego autem nihil tale* (as the reprehensible sins of the Presbyter Valens) *sensi in vobis vel audivi, in quibus laboravit beatus Paulus, qui estis in principio epistulae (v. I. ecclesiae) eius. De vobis etenim gloriatur in omnibus ecclesiis, quae deum solae tunc cognoverant; nos autem nondum noveramus.* One sees here a reminiscence of 2 Thess 1:4: ὥστε αὐτοὺς ἡμᾶς ἐν ὑμῖν ἐγκαυχᾶσθαι ἐν ταῖς ἐκκλησίαις τοῦ θεοῦ. One then assumes that Polycarp has mistakenly believed that this verse is found in Paul's Letter to the Philippians or he has (knowingly) at the start "combined" the related communities of Philippi and Thessalonica with regard to their geographical location and the history of their Christian mission.[23] A third possibility would be that Polycarp was not thinking about 2 Thess 1:4 but considered here other passages such as 2 Cor 8:1–24 and Rom 15:26 where one speaks not about Philippi but about Macedonia, and then would have unknowingly formed the expression according to 2 Thess 1:4. To the contrary, such an assumption would be artificial. Then again the view that one is dealing here with a mix-up or confusion is distinctly dubious in a letter to the Philippians. It appears that the third possibility—that Polycarp has somehow combined Thessalonica and Philippi—is the correct solution. On its own, one must concede that it is certainly not easy to imagine that someone who is writing to the Philippians and who has this specific community in mind should have simply transferred and conveyed statements and assertions about the Thessalonians to them. Thus one would then be prompted to place the entire premise that Polycarp has created this expression of his from 2 Thess 1:4 in doubt. Yet alone the correctness of this assumption— and that in itself is what interests us with this matter—thrusts itself to the

---

23. Zahn, *Die Geschichte des Kanons*, 815–17. This is his opinion in his work on the history of the canon. He seeks to explain the plural, ἐπιστολαί, on the basis of Polycarp's *Letter to the Philippians*, Pol 3:2. He understands Pol, *Phil* 1:2 to be an allusion to 1 Thess 1:8–9. Besides that he ascribes to the view that in the ancient biblical writings the *Letter to the Philippians* either followed and was joined to the letters to the Thessalonians or they preceded it altogether. (Cf. *Geschichte des Kanons*, 3, 49, 353ff) Zahn favors the acceptance of the confusion in the edition of the *Patr. Apost.* (11:3). An earlier explanation can be found in his work, *Ignatius von Antiochien*, 505.

contrary upon us once more. The *gloriari in ecclesiis* is rather peculiar usage, and furthermore the *de vobis* corresponds well with ἐν ὑμῖν.[24]

Thus I submit that Polycarp well knew and was familiar with our letter. The appropriateness of this date certainly corresponds with the date given for the composition of the Letter of Polycarp. However, I cannot present the research for this here. Further beyond the date that Harnack[25] last suggested from around AD 110 to 117 or perhaps several years later from AD 117 to 125 is not a serious consideration, and one will definitely not date the letter from any time later than that. If then we take this determination as a basis, so then under all circumstances the time around the turn of the century remains open, possibly even up to the time around AD 110. But the situation can be better and even clearer characterized and determined. Polycarp's use of the First Letter to Timothy can be documented not with any less certainty but with even more clarity than his use of our letter to the Thessalonians as namely the comparison of Poly 4:1 and 1 Tim 6:7, 10 demonstrates. Therefore the following can be stated: under the presupposition that Polycarp has used the letter, it need not have been written earlier than the First Letter to Timothy for this letter was certainly not written before the end of the first century.

All of these considerations are superfluous and irrelevant if the verse about the Anti-Christ in the remark of 2 Thess 2:4 presupposes the existence of the Jerusalem Temple at the time of the composition of the letter. It has previously been recognized that in this case a falsified Second Letter to the Thessalonians can hardly at all be perceived and recognized. Is therefore our entire exegetical presentation to be ultimately discarded with this passage about the Temple?[26] One will proceed with the immediate review of the full impact of this question with the conclusion of our study.

---

24. Harnack, *Patristische Miscellen*, 86ff. I refer to Harnack's work which has substantially advanced the understanding of this difficult and clearly corrupt passage. Harnack initially takes Zahn's interpretation above, but then discards the admittedly objectionable *omnibus* (before *ecclesiis*) and combines it with *vobis*. He thus assumes in the improbable relative clause, *qui estis in principio epistulae eius*, a *landati* before the *estis*, so that the *in principio epistulae eius* then refers to the beginning of the Second Letter to the Thessalonians, specifically to 2 Thess 1:4. The question remains though if the *omnibus* is to be explained on the basis of 2 Thess 1:3 as Harnack presumes.

25. Harnack, *Chronologie*, 406.

26. Brückner, *Die chronologische Reihenfolge*, 255–56. Brückner places the Second Letter to the Thessalonians after the First Letter of Peter and the Book of Revelation. He presupposes a fictional address just I have done, but he then does not lose one word with a most exaggerated, chronological appraisal of 2 Thess 2:4 that is most astonishing.

CHAPTER V

THE SIGNIFICANCE OF THE JERUSALEM TEMPLE

Those scholars who have believed that the letter should be dated after the year AD 70 have previously helped their cause by assuming that with 2 Thess 2:4 the word ναός has a figurative meaning. The writer here intended and refers to the spiritual Temple of Christianity. The entire proclamation that the Anti-Christ will seat himself in the Temple of God is intended to point where possible to the culmination of the heresy of Gnosticism.[1] But with this understanding of ναὸς τοῦ θεοῦ one makes the statement a far too easy matter. Such a view is surely suitable for the allegories of the Church Fathers[2] and good also for Hengstenberg,[3] but much less suitable for modern scholars. One can namely present a long list of parallels.[4] But they do

---

1. Bahnsen, *Jahrbücher*, 696ff.; Hilgenfeld, *Einleitung*, 650ff.; *Zeitschrift*, 253; Pfleiderer, *Das Urchristentum*, 397. Pfleiderer certainly does not express himself with regard to the "Temple."

2. Bornemann, *Die Thessalonicherbriefe*, 406, 410; Malvenda, *De Antichristo*, 61. For example Chrysostomus, Hieronymous, and with his rather strange interpretation Augustine thought about and considered the Church of God. The view of Theodoret, Theophylact among others that the Temple of God designates the churches cannot really be related and placed alongside that other (first) concept because the churches are the buildings and basilicas. This interpretation is not allegorical.

3. Hengstenberg, *Die Offenbarung*, 548, 558ff. He refers to Rev 11:1ff.

4. Hilgenfeld, *Einleitung*, 650. He cites and quotes from 1 Cor 3:16–17; 2 Cor 6:16; Heb 3:6; 10:21; 1 Pet 2:5; 4:17; 1 Tim 3:15; *1 Clem* 23. Only the last passage may not be compared to 2 Thess 2:4; more about this on 100 below.

not prove anything collectively for our case. They require quite explicitly that the word temple should be understood in figurative sense, but then usually they allow for this meaning to be specified at once. That aspect of the verse that makes a reference to the church impossible is assuredly not just the double definite article (εἰς τὸν ναὸν τοῦ θεοῦ).[5] Certainly no writer who wanted to express the idea that the Anti-Christ will appear in the church or will invade or intrude into the church would have made use of the phrase καθίσαι εἰς τὸν ναὸν τοῦ θεοῦ.[6] Above all the concept of the church does not suit the context of this passage at all. With the phrase, ὥστε εἰς τὸν ναὸν τοῦ θεοῦ καθίσαι, it is clear that the matter concerns a demonstration for the sacrilegious arrogance of the Anti-Christ to the extent that without any timidity he grasps for the highest dignity. In the proposal that he offensively reaches for and strikes, the Holy One is blotted out but can nonetheless be discerned in the background. If the church should have been meant here rather than the most Holy Sanctuary, the actual sacred site where God is found and is enthroned, so then the phrase εἰς τὸν ναὸν τοῦ θεοῦ loses its proper tone. If one replaces this expression with the rather putative concept of "Christianity," "the Church of God," then one will sense the difference. For to intrude or make one's way into the church is not at all a sign of sacrilegious self-exaltation.

We must begin with the candid acknowledgment that the interpretation of these words for the Jerusalem Temple are not in any event not scandalous, but are to be exclusively considered here since the writer himself has formed and molded this visionary conception. Such an endeavor would also result because of several other reasons. For the consequence is hardly to be avoided that the Jerusalem Temple still stood when the writer wrote this passage. It is a fact that world events that occur almost everyday and even those that lie in the immediate past are not known to people who should know about them. But that a literate Christian who lived around the turn of the first century should have known nothing about the destruction of Jerusalem is not at all credible.

Yet the question remains as to whether or not it is a different matter if the writer took the remark about the Anti-Christ from another source that states that the Anti-Christ was to seat himself in God's Temple. But also in

---

5. Bornemann, *Die Thessalonicherbriefe*, z. St.

6. Baur, *Paulus*, 358. The same reason argues strongly against Baur's probable and otherwise hardly mentioned viewpoint that with the εἰς τὸν ναὸν τοῦ θεοῦ actually the τόπος τοῦ ναοῦ has been designated, the ground and ruins of the destroyed Temple which are also considered to be holy just as the prior Temple itself.

this case the first and most immediate thought with an isolated observation of this eschatological passage is certainly that the Jerusalem Temple and namely the existing Temple has been referred to. From the outset we will not set our expectations too high. The passage itself in any case does not explicitly demonstrate anything but the possibility of another viewpoint.

Another perception could lead either to the fact that the writer with regard to this questionable usage does not need to consider the actual, concrete Jerusalem Temple at all because he has taken it over from another source; or on the other hand that although the Jerusalem Temple had been destroyed at the time he wrote these words, he could still have made use of this concept. Can one seriously consider one or the other of these two possibilities?

The preliminary question asks if it is at all possible that the writer himself has not formed the thought and image that the Anti-Christ will seat himself in God's Temple but rather if it is possible that he has taken it over from another source. This question is to be answered positively, and I emphasize here not because it is convenient for our point of view but because it is completely independent from the matter which concerns us most.

That the writer for the most part in chapter 2 has not presented apocalyptic ideas and images of his own view and contrivance is well agreed to and accepted today.[7] Expressions such as ὁ ἄνθρωπος τῆς ἁμαρτίας, ἡ ἀποστασία, ὁ κατέχων, and τὸ κατέχον appear according to the text to be terms that have been previously coined. The parallels that occur for many aspects and characteristics of the presentation give us a further confirmation. I have already remarked above[8] that the description gives us much more than the obvious motive itself allows, namely the question about when the Day of the Lord will come. It is very likely that the search for an explanation of this lies in the fact that the writer was bound by a picture or image that had already been described with definite characteristics.

Spitta has presumed that there was a written source, and to be sure, not just a general one. Much more rather he has advanced the precise hypothesis that a Jewish-apocalyptic discourse from the time of Caligula has been taken over by Timothy—who he assumes was the writer—in his documented letter,[9] but assuredly with a reinterpretation of the original

---

7. Bousset, *Der Antichrist*, 13ff.; Gunkel, *Schöpfung und Chaos*, 221ff.: Spitta, *Zur Geschichte*, 139; Zahn, *Einleitung*, 162.

8. See 40–41 above.

9. We add here 2 Thess 3:1ff. so that all that reminds us of 1 Thess 3:8—4:2 will be

meaning.¹⁰ However totally independent of the question of the writer, I cannot follow and accept this hypothesis.¹¹ Only one meager aspect, just the καθίσαι εἰς τὸν ναὸν τοῦ θεοῦ, can even point to and awaken the thought of Caligula. The emperor intended to erect a colossal statue of himself in the Jerusalem Temple and his proposal called forth the most profound rage and uproar among the Jewish people.¹² But nothing in the entire passage refers to the emperor and that would be very strange and unusual for a "Caligula-Apocalypse." Moreover the entire portrait does not have any political character whatsoever, and an earthly ruler has not been described here. It may be especially added that no explanation can be found and assumed for the κατέχων according to this conception.¹³ Meanwhile even the relationship to Caligula is by no means evident, for the matter of erecting his statue in the Temple is at the start something rather different than that of seating himself in it.¹⁴ To identify both without factual circumstances will thus advise against the acceptance of such a view, for there are related thoughts aspects in the passage that clearly have nothing to do with Caligula.¹⁵

Nonetheless it cannot be ruled out that the writer, be it with the entire passage or in small segments of his description, has been influenced by a written source unknown to us.¹⁶ Such is by no means impossible precisely

---

placed side by side.

10. Spitta, *Zur Geschichte*, 134–49; *Die Offenbarung*, 497–500.

11. Gunkel, *Schöpfung und Chaos*, 221ff.

12. Schürer, *Geschichte*, 495ff, 503ff.

13. Holtzmann, *Einleitung*, 216; Spitta, *Offenbarung*, 499; *Zur Geschichte*, 139ff, 146ff. Spitta names Aristobul, the brother of Herod Agrippa, as well as Agrippa himself and Vitellius according to the view of Grotius. In the reinterpretation of the original Apocalypse of John which was made by Timothy, Claudius was considered to be the κατέχων. Originally the image of the winning and dominating schemes of Caligula should have corresponded to the agitation caused by the μυστήριον τῆς ἀνομίας.

14. Bousset, *Der Antichrist*; Gunkel, *Schöpfung und Chaos*; Kern, "Über 2 Thess 2:1–12," 189. Kern has opposed Grotius.

15. Bousset, *Der Antichrist*, 14, 104, 106; Bousset, *Kommentar zur Apokalypse*, 58; Victorin, *Apokalypsenkommentar*. At a later date a variation of this expectation can certainly be documented that directly reminds one of Caligula. Bousset has referred to this on the pages listed above. Victorin states the following about Rev 13:15: *faciet etiam* (the false prophet), *ut imago aurea anticrhisto in templo Hierosolymis ponatur*. Bousset assumes that this expectation arose during Caligula's lifetime, but that is not very probable from my point of view.

16. Bousset, *Der Antichrist*, 6; Schmiedel, Untitled Entry, *Handkommentar*, 41. On page 6 Bousset postulates an "existing, written prophecy that was already known to Paul." Others such as Michelsen have considered a written original text.

The Significance of the Jerusalem Temple

because he gives an answer to the question concerning the time for the Parousia that contains far more than an answer and which is not entirely clear and understandable viewed from the vantage point of his own polemical purpose. It would not at all contradict that matter itself if he makes his distinct opinion known in this section. He would then have made use of his source according to the specific standpoint which he considered most important and yet at the same time would have retained his own view that was not dependent on the source. Certainly then for that reason because he has subordinated the entire theme of the Anti-Christ to the question of coming of the Last Judgment, it is definite that he is not simply a writer who has possibly copied an original text. The remark of 2 Thess 2:5 leads to the same thought and concept that reminds us of the earlier teaching of Paul to the Thessalonians, followed by the οἴδατε of 2 Thess 2:6, all of which establishes the style of his imitation of the First Letter to the Thessalonians. Again, there is no necessity to consider a written source. But with such a consideration one cannot assert anything more than the possibility.

The special expectation that the Anti-Christ might seat himself in the Temple of God has certainly not yet been documented in the earliest apocalyptic literature. Admittedly though the words of Mark 13:14, ὅταν δὲ ἴδητε τὸ βδέλυγμα τῆς ἐρημώσεως ἑστηκότα ὅπου οὐ δεῖ, could well be considered to be a complete parallel. The presupposition that the masculine constructed participle of βδέλυγμα points to the Anti-Christ is very attractive. It is certain that one is thinking here of a person, a human figure rather than the Roman army.[17] However, complete certainly is difficult to attain here because of the indefinite use of the expression ὅπου οὐ δεῖ. A hill or mound as a place of a high altar can hardly be found in the numerous occurrences of the idea of a hill that appear in the church fathers or in the later ecclesiastical, apocalyptic literature.[18] Actually it appears that the most likely explanation is just the text of 2 Thess 2:4 itself that provides the characteristic trait and then confirms and disseminates it, and which in the meantime has become holy writ.

Nonetheless the thought and concept will be even less dependent on the personal view of the writer than on the content of the little apocalypse in its entirety. The apocalypse does not appear to occur here as something

---

17. Bousset, *Der Antichrist*, 14, 141–42; Holtzmann, Untitled Entry, *Handkommentar*, 168; Klostermann, *Das Markusevangelium*, 252; Zahn, *Einleitung*, 168. Bousset also understands this expression from Matt 24:15 in the same way: βδέλυγμα τῆς ἐρημώσεως. However, that appears rather difficult to me.

18. Bousset, *Der Antichrist*, 104–5.

new, and one cannot easily conjecture that the writer might have created it just casually from free fantasy. One may add that related concepts and images in Judaism just as well as in early Jewish Christianity have been documented many times.[19] The epitome of such sacrilegious pretentiousness can already be found in Isa 14:13–14 and Ezek 28:2[20] where pagan kings make themselves equal to the highest being or place themselves on the same level as God. Naturally that word from our passage itself quoted from Dan 11:36–37 concerning the exaltation of sacrilegious kings over every God belongs to this list, and with a somewhat different meaning also all words about the βδέλυγμα τῆς ἐρημώσεως from Daniel and the books of the Maccabees.[21] Furthermore according to Daniel 6, Darius tempted and misled when he issued the commandment that no one would be permitted to make a petition to any other god or person other than himself. According to Jdt 3:8 Holofernes wants to destroy all of the gods of the earth so that only Nebuchadnezzar can be called upon as the supreme god (cf. Jdt 6:2). Because he plunders and destroys the holy sanctuaries of the people (Jdt 4:1), one also fears the desecration and profanation of the Jerusalem Temple as reported in Jdt 4:2; 8:21; 9:2. Obviously this concern is related to belief in the divination of kings. Thus the characteristic theme from 3 Macc 1:8—2:24 deserves to be mentioned here, whereby the pagan king Ptolemy exalts himself and has the audacity to enter the Holy of Holies.[22] Along with the description of the first animal in the Book of Revelation it is stated in chapter 13 that one should pray to the animal so that it be made a god (Rev 13:4, 12) and that this same animal blasphemes the name of God and his tent (Rev 13:5–6) with its mouth of a great capacity. But finally one should admittedly remember here the relationship to the scheme that Caligula proposed.

19. Gunkel, *Schöpfung und Chaos*, 221–22.

20. Ezek 28:2 LXX reads as follows: Καὶ σύ, υἱὲ ἀνθρώπου, εἰπὸν τῷ ἄρχοντι Τύρου Τάδε λέγει κύριος Ἀνθ᾽ οὗ ὑψώθη σου ἡ καρδία καὶ εἶπας Θεός εἰμι ἐγώ, κατοικίαν θεοῦ κατοίκηκα ἐν καρδίᾳ θαλάσσης, σὺ δὲ εἶ ἄνθρωπος καὶ οὐ θεός κτλ. Cf. also Ezek 28:6, 9. One could be inclined to to derive the mention of the Temple in 2 Thess 2:4 directly from this verse and other similar, related passages, but such an assertion is most difficult to substantiate. Hippolytus has already related this verse to the Antichrist, but then later with 2 Thess 2:4 he was presumably reminded of that. Cf. Malvenda, *De Antichristo*, c, 53: μετὰ ταῦτα ἄρξεται ὡς θεὸν ἐπιδεικνύμαι, ὡς προεῖπεν Ἐζεκιηλ· ἀνθ᾽ ὧν ὑψώθη ἡ καρδία σου, καὶ εἶπας· Θεὸς εἰμι ἐγώ.

21. Dan 8:11–12, 9:27, 11:31, 12:11; 1 Macc 1:54ff. etc.

22. The story of Heliodorus, the Chancellor of Seleukus, taken from 2 Macc 3:9ff. is related to this matter.

The Significance of the Jerusalem Temple

The premises for the concepts of our passage, the assassination of the true God, the usurpation of divine dignity, and the violation of the divine Temple are accordingly to be found in a previous Jewish milieu, for our passage undeniably and uniquely contains these elements in a special combination and relationship. It appears to me that if Paul could be considered to be the writer of this letter, it would be most probable to find this characteristic trait about the expectation of the Anti-Christ as an element of an older tradition. Thereby it must remain an entirely other matter as to whether or not it can be ascribed to Paul at a later date; not that he took it over and held strongly to it, but that he brought it forth on his own. It would thus be considered as a characteristic trait about which one is not able to assert anything certain other than it emerged from Paul's consciousness for which the Temple possessed a decisive meaning and import (i.e., a specific Jewish consciousness).[23] Should the uproar about Caligula have rubbed off on and colored the expectation of the Anti-Christ and thus produced the image of 2 Thess 2:4,[24] we would then be directed under all circumstances to a time for its origin that still freshly sensed that agitation.

Thus we hold it to be definitely probable that these words have come from a much older source and tradition, and from now on we will consider them based on this premise.

May we then assume that the writer could reinterpret the ναὸς τοῦ θεοῦ to refer to the church of Christianity? This opinion must be assuredly repudiated once more. One could namely perhaps refer to *1 Clem* 23:5 as a parallel. When furthermore the verse from Mal 3:1, ἐξαίφνης ἥξει εἰς τὸν ναὸν ἑαυτοῦ κύριος καὶ ὁ ἅγιος ὃν ὑμεῖς προσδοκᾶτε, is quoted as a reference to the Second Coming of Christ, one can hardly have meant the Temple of Jerusalem unless it might appear that the εἰς τὸν ναὸν τοῦ θεοῦ has tacitly been reinterpreted. It is more probable that the Temple has not at all been definitely referred to, for all of the emphasis lies with the concept of the coming Parousia. But the assumption of a reinterpretation here would definitely not have the difficulty our passage itself has, because it would already deal with a fixed quotation taken from the text. If the writer wanted despite

---

23. Bousset, *Der Antichrist*, 107. cf. 93. Bousset's presupposition that the last origin of this characteristic concept is to be found in the myth of the dragon—the Temple would initially have been conceived of as the heavenly home of God—could perhaps remain alongside this imagery. However to date it does not seem to me to have become probable. The concept that the Anti-Christ is to seat himself in the Temple of God in and of itself does not contain any characteristic that points beyond a Jewish milieu.

24. So also Zahn. The view of Grotius has been substantiated.

the καθίσαι to understand 2 Thess 2:4 based on the phrase, ναὸς τοῦ θεοῦ, as Christianity itself, so he would have made his opinion known with an additional comment or a definite reference. Moreover it still remains even here that for this relationship the concept of the church is not at all suitable.[25]

Another kind of reinterpretation might certainly be considered. If the precept of ναὸς τοῦ θεοῦ has not been allegorized, so then the entire καθίσαι εἰς τὸν ναὸν τοῦ θεοῦ could have become the primary image. The usage would then only mean that the Anti-Christ claims for himself the place of God or that he demands to be God for all of the people. Von Hofmann defended this explanation, although he was not beset by concern or reservation about the time of the composition or the Pauline origin of the letter. Because the Pauline expression is related to and follows closely Isa 14:13–14 and Ezek 28:2, "the question as to whether or not the Temple of God could be understood as the stone Temple of Jerusalem, a present or a future Temple, or the Church of Christianity" might not at all "be prompted or called for."[26] The matter actually concerns only what the Anti-Christ will declare himself to represent, but nothing about his explanation of the action or consequences such an explanation entails. According to this then the words ἀποδεικνύντα ἑαυτὸν ὅτι ἐστὶν θεός must specify what the εἰς τὸν ναὸν τοῦ θεοῦ καθίσαι consists of or by what it is confirmed. Thus these words must provide the real understanding of the figurative expression.[27] But that by itself does not correlate their immediate impression. Rather it appears distinctly on the opposite hand that with εἰς τὸν ναὸν τοῦ θεοῦ καθίσαι a concrete action has been given that either forms and provides the prerequisite for the ἀποδεικνύναι or that it itself already contains it, so that the words ἀποδεικνύντα ἑαυτὸν κτλ still emphasize only something that already lies in the previous primary assertion and declaration. Furthermore it can be added that the usage of the phrase, "to seat oneself in the Temple of God," by no means appears to be or reminds one of a mere image or picture or even much less a proverbial colloquialism that would mean "to

---

25. Cf. 94 above.

26. Bornemann, *Die Thessalonicherbriefe*, 669. Cf. his report on the comments of Baumgarten-Crusius; Kern, "Über 2 Thess 2:1–12," 158. He opposes such a conclusion; Schott, *Epistolae Pauli ad Thessalonicenses et Galatas*. His similar explanation precedes that of von Hoffmann's as he wrote around 1834; von Hoffmann, *Die heilige Schrift*, 315.

27. The ἀποδεικνύντα ἑαυτὸν with ὅτι in fact does not need to mean anything more than that the Antichrist "indeed explains and proclaims that he himself, namely he in opposition to the true and veritable God, is God" (von Hoffmann). The significance of "to display or unveil oneself" does not need to be considered.

seat oneself on God's place or seat." Yet from the perspective of our presupposition that the writer has reproduced a much older concept, perhaps the matter could be more easily presented from a clearer vantage point. But on its own merit we do not need to pursue that. The writer must knowingly have actually given the original and real meaning of this usage with what he wrote. But then one asks once more: Why does he not make the understanding of it clear?

The relationship to the actual Temple of Jerusalem cannot be excluded from the passage. Thus there remain only two possibilities.[28] Either the writer must have made the silent presupposition that the Temple that has already been destroyed will be built anew in the last days, or he must have taken the report that the Anti-Christ will seat himself in the Temple of God from another source, simply because it had been preserved and handed on like that.

With the first case we would have a plain and unquestionable solution to the difficulty. But can we ascribe to the writer the expectation that the Temple is to be restored?

If with his composition of the letter he had fostered this notion and if he had written with the definite memory that the Temple at that time had been destroyed, so very likely he would probably have divulged that with a specific intimation and elucidating comment. In and of itself that remains outright a ponderous objection. For no one will believe that he purposely wanted to awaken the impression that the Temple still stands so that one does not assume that he writes after Paul's time. But there are other matters that speak against such an expectation of the writer.

One assuredly cannot assert that a Christian who lived around the turn of the century could not have expected the renewal of the earthly Jerusalem. It would for that reason be very possible that he accordingly anticipated the rebuilding of the Temple because with certainty Judaism and the Jewish people expected that after AD 70. For it cannot be assumed that one would have to disallow such an expectation because of the antagonism against the Jewish cult. But what does the Anti-Christ have to do with such chiliastic expectation? The renewal of Jerusalem would still not have been completed with the coming of the Ani-Christ.

---

28. Schürer, *Geschichte*, I, 537, 640; II, 546; III, 99. It would not help to consider the Temple of Leontopolis and to displace the writer to Egypt, since the Temple of Jerusalem was already closed by the Romans in AD 73.

The Authenticity of the Second Letter to the Thessalonians

In the writings of the Church Fathers, we encounter the belief that the Temple of Jerusalem will be rebuilt and that thereafter the Anti-Christ will seat himself in it.[29] But it is rather the opinion at least generally as a rule that the Anti-Christ himself will rebuild the Temple,[30] and thereby manifest his zeal for the Jewish civilization. Parallel to this is the concept that either he will raise up the Jewish kingdom to please the Jewish people or that he will restore the Jewish rituals (i.e., Temple worship. B. Primasius[31] says for example: *Nam templum Hierosolymis restitute et omnia legis caeremonialia restaurabit*). But equivalent anti-Jewish tendencies can be documented with Hippolytus[32] in corresponding passages. Thus it does not require any proof that this specific expectation of the restoration of the Temple has nothing to do with the origin of the same Jewish expectation, but rather that it has been solely formed and conceived in a relationship with a later expectation of the Anti-Christ and for no other reason than to conform with the verse 2 Thess 2:4. This Pauline prophecy, the sacrosanct word of the Apostle, could to be sure not remain unfulfilled. If the Anti-Christ was thus to sit in the Temple of God, so then he himself must build it anew. If this understanding and concept was once prevalent among Christian theologians, so it need not have necessarily been repeated every time when the sacrilege of the ἄνομος was mentioned. Therefore it is surely remarkable but not at all incomprehensible that Irenaeus,[33] for example, often speaks about this fact that the Anti-Christ will sit in the Temple, and most assuredly in the Jerusalem Temple, without mentioning in this relationship even one word about its restoration.[34] Thus he can well have been familiar with this postulate that was derived from 2 Thess 2:4.

But for our writer this is an entirely different matter than that of the Church Fathers; and so we cannot assume that as he wrote, he actually thought about the restoration of the Temple.

---

29. Bornemann, *Die Thessalonicherbriefe*, 405; Bousset, *Der Antichrist*, 105; Malvenda, *De Antichristo*, p 61 sq.

30. A variation on this expectation is that the Jewish people will build the Temple for the Antichrist.

31. Malvenda, *De Antichristo*, l c.

32. Ibid., c 6, 54. Cf. Malvenda and also 25 in Danielem IV 49.

33. Irenaeus, *Adv. Haer.*, V 25. Cf. also V 28:2, 30:4.

34. In a later context with V 34, 35 the theme concerns the "*reaedificatio*" of Jerusalem. This "*Hierusalem reaedificata*" is not however the Jerusalem that the Antichrist enters.

The Significance of the Jerusalem Temple

Let us examine the other possibility that the writer propagated the concept of the Anti-Christ who seats himself in the Temple without at all considering the destruction of the Temple and without any clear understanding or sense of the contradiction entailed by the fact and tradition of this prophecy.

The tenacity of the apocalyptic tradition handed on to us has recently been distinctly called to our attention. It is not an impossible or unusual occurrence that characteristics of an earlier apocalyptic expectation have been preserved despite the fact that they are no longer understood, and that apocalyptic images remain untouched and not fully understood, although the relationships and situations for which they were initially intended should have required modifications.[35] But 2 Thess 2:4 does not express anything incomprehensible, nor does it present imagery that would have been interpreted or employed and adopted for the first time. Here rather it is much more the case that an image has been preserved according to an earlier meaning and its import, albeit that this image may have become impossible in this sense because of a well-known event. Without doubt, therefore, what one anticipates at the start is that the writer would either have stripped the image of its earlier meaning or that he would have provided a clear and pertinent interpretation.

This expectation appears to be even less disallowed when one considers the context. With 2 Thess 2:6 the writer writes: καὶ νῦν τὸ κατέχον οἴδατε. Thus this κατέχον presents a clear dimension of well-known importance to its readers. By means of this, the impression arises that one is dealing in this entire contextual relationship with a rather lively and understandable tradition. Yet we hardly anticipate a characteristic aspect that just like a prehistoric fossil would exclude itself from the earlier tradition.

Nonetheless this consideration can be compared to others. If a Pseudo-Paul is speaking here, so with the οἴδατε one will by no means be able to tap actual assets and understanding. If holding to the fiction and following up[36] on it he had said, "Do you not remember that I told you all of that when I was with you?", then he should be able to easily add a further explanation about the κατέχον[37] as a matter that was already known to the readers. It

---

35. Bousset, *Der Antichrist*, 40; Gunkel, *Schöpfung und Chaos*, 282, 335, 344 etc.

36. See 62 above.

37. Here I am not going to elaborate on the meaning of the expressions κατέχον and ὁ κατέχων. It is from my point of view not very probable that the usual interpretation that has been advanced by the oldest exegetical tradition is correct according to which the variation from neuter to masculine is to be explained by the reflection about the Roman

would have certainly been baffling if he had said that the readers first of all should have recently come to an understanding of κατέχον (νῦν—οἴδατε). How would the writer have come to falsify the opposition and paradox between an earlier and present knowledge of the matter? Such a proclamation must necessarily have had a definite cause and reason. Alone by itself the νῦν has nothing to do with the οἴδατε, for at least logically it belongs together with the κατέχον (i.e., it has not been meant to distinguish between an understanding attained in the present from something not known or understood at an earlier time). It can have only characterized the "delay" as a matter of the present in opposition to the future. At the present the coming of the Anti-Christ has been obstructed, but (ἐν τῷ αὐτοῦ καιρῷ) later he will reveal himself to the world. Thus then with this interpretation[38] the καὶ οἴδατε is to be viewed as the simple continuation of the οὐ μνημονεύετε, for this is to be directly understood from the fictional situation. Any special conclusions concerning the current, vital expectations and understanding of the recently imparted eschatological tradition cannot be ascertained from this passage.

The presentation of the writer is coherent and free of any confusion. Still that certainly does not favor the assumption that with his mention of the Temple the writer might have retained a trace or traits of a much older tradition without having qualified it in light of the obvious objection concerning it.

Thus, one searches for analogies that might be able to shed some light on this existing usage and report. The prospect of being able to provide

---

Empire and its personal emperors.

38. Bornemann, *Die Thessalonicherbriefe*; von Hoffmann, *Die heilige Schrift*; Zahn, *Eiinleitung*, 168. Each of these scholars to be sure advances this interpretation albeit in a somewhat different manner. I consider Zahn's view of the actual combination of νῦν with κατέχον to be permissible. Cf. the parallels to 2 Thess 2:7: ὁ κατέχων ἄρτι. Biblical criticism has for the most part held the other view according to which νῦν οἴδατε as opposed to ἔτι ὢν πρὸς ὑμᾶς of 2 Thess 2:5 might refer to the earliest knowledge given to the people. But it has thereby not regarded the factual difficulites that precisely proscribe this interpretation. The most recently imparted notification could not be mere fiction, for such instruction could only be an actual fact. Should the oppositional statement ἔτι ὢν κτλ pertain to something that is fictional? That would be even more strange and unusual! Furthermore when the Pseudo-Paul presupposes that his readers already know about the κατέχων, then therein it is readily clear that the teaching and expectation about the Antichrist is also fresh in their memory. For it is obvious that the κατέχων even requires and assumes the Antichrist. Thus the entire teaching of this expectation would either not have any purpose or it must have been rather differently conceived of and formulated from another perspective.

such evidence is certainly not good. For seldom in any other case would such an eschatological expectation be similarly related to such a chronology (i.e., it is not very likely that such an expectation would be alluded to in early Christianity by means of a generally well-known and epoch-making event such that the Anti-Christ will seat himself in the Jerusalem Temple and bring about thereby the destruction of the Temple). Yet meanwhile there could be other comparable cases and events that deal directly with the Temple.

At any event one is perhaps reminded here of those passages in the early Christian and Jewish literature in which after the year AD 70 blood sacrifice and thus the Temple are mentioned in the present tense as if they still existed.[39] The early scholarship found in some of these writings evidence for the composition of the respective written report of the destruction of the Jerusalem Temple.[40] Namely *I Clem* 41 is to be read accordingly in its entirety as though the Temple cult still existed.[41] Furthermore, who knows how one would understand these words today if rather than in the *First Letter of Clement* they occurred in the texts of the Letter to the Ephesians or the Letter to the Colossians. But on the contrary one cannot speak at all here about a parallel to our text and situation. Certainly though just with this passage from the *First Letter of Clement*, it is not without interest that the thought and concept of the destiny of Jerusalem that appears to us to be so imminent is not by any means apparent to the writer. On its own the use of the present tense can be easily explained as it is generally acknowledged today: it is not the historical circumstances that float and wave before the view of the writer but rather the conceptual lasting and perpetual legal provisions of the Old Testament.

---

39. 1 *Clem* c 41; *Epist ad Diogn* c 3; Friedmann and Grätz, *Die angebliche Fordauer*, 338ff.; cf. Harnack on *1 Clem* 41; Josephus, *Antiquitt*, III 6–12, *Contra Apionem* 1:7, 2:6 fin, 2:23 (where the future appears alongside the present); Justin Martyr, *Dialogue*, 117; Schürer, *Geschichte*, 548ff, 652ff. See also rabbinical sources.

40. Hefele, *Patr Apost Opp*, XXXVI: He believes for example that without the existence of the Temple Clement's entire argument would be invalid; Josephus, *Antiquit*, III 6–12. He has decided against Clement's argument.; Otto, *De Epistola ad Diognetum*, 14; Tillemont, *Der Brief an Diognet*, c 3; Uhlhorn, *Niedners Zeitschrift*, 322. Uhlhorn comes to a similar conclusion as that of Josephus. Tillemont has dated the Letter to Diognetus before AD 70 on the basis of c 3. Cf. Otto and his work on the Letter to Diognetus. Finally one must remember the Letter to the Hebrews.

41. 1 *Clem* 41:2: Οὐ πανταχοῦ, ἀδελφοί, προσφέρονται θυσίαι ἐνδελεχισμοῦ ἢ εὐχῶν ἢ περὶ ἁμαρτίας καὶ πλημμελείας, ἀλλ᾽ ἢ ἐν Ἱερουσαλὴμ μόνῃ· κἀκεῖ δὲ οὐκ ἐν παντὶ τόπῳ προσφέρεται, ἀλλ᾽ ἔμπροσθεν τοῦ ναοῦ πρὸς τὸ θυσιαστήριον κτλ.

The Authenticity of the Second Letter to the Thessalonians

On the other hand, the Apocalypse of John offers some words that one can with more justification draw on for a better comparison. Verses 1 and 2 of chapter 11 of the Apocalypse of John report that the visionary has been summoned to measure the Temple of God and the altar, to count the people praying there, but to omit and pass over the outer courtyard: "for it was given only to the Gentiles and they will tread upon the Holy City forty-two months long."

By all means it deserves to be mentioned that the same difficulties arise here, the same attempts at interpretation, and the same considerations that we encounter when we follow the equivalent words and expressions of the Second Letter to the Thessalonians. More often than not it is also this passage that is viewed to be the clear and compelling evidence for the composition of the Apocalypse before the year AD 70.[42] Yet the ναὸς τοῦ θεοῦ has had great appeal as a later allegorical interpretation in favor of a much later dating of the book, even up to the modern era.[43] Furthermore the hypothesis has been offered that the prophecy refers to the rebuilding of the Temple.[44] Most scholars today will ascribe to the view that an already outdated and obsolete prophecy has been taken over and alluded to here, one that arose prior to these events. For the image has been conceived that the Temple will remain and be preserved in a time of adversity, as for example during asylum, undoubtedly at a time during which the Temple still stood.[45] On the other hand, however, with regard to definite indications and evidence, the Apocalypse in its entirety could have first originated at a much later time.

---

42. Düsterdieck, *Kommentar*; Bleek, *Einleitung*, 722–23. Their views may be compared on this topic.

43. Bousset, *Kommentar zur Offenbarung*; Hengstenberg, *Die Offenbarung*; Beyschlag; Weiss, *Einleitung*, 367. Hengstenberg is of the opinion that the Temple refers to the Church. Weiss has a similar view as that of Beyschlag who sees here a reference to the observant Jewish community. Cf. Bousset's point of view.

44. Wabnitz, Untitled Entry, *Jahrbuch*, 134, 512; Zahn, *Die Geschichte*, 591, 597, 594, 600, 618, 621. Zahn assumes that Rev 11:1–2 refers to a time in which the Temple has already been destroyed and that the saving restoration of the Temple is to occur during the "time of the Antichrist." He does not address the matter as to how the writer can have conceived of the Temple as still standing after the year AD 70. It appears that though in another manner than that of Wabnitz he also ascribes to the expectation of a future restoration of the Temple.

45. Bousset, *Kommentar*, 373; Gunkel, *Schöpfung und Chaos*, 219–20. I rather doubt along with Gunkel that this imagery and expectation arose precisely at the time of the beginning of the siege of Jerusalem by the Roman army. Cf. Bousset, 373. The forty-two months can be understood to argue against such a view, i.e., the number 3 ½.

THE SIGNIFICANCE OF THE JERUSALEM TEMPLE

If we follow this argument, so one will certainly have to ask as Bousset[46] has done how the writer of the Apocalypse could have taken over a much older prophecy and what he must have intended and thought with such a use of the older tradition. Bousset conjectured that the writer viewed the measurement of the Temple not as a sign of its preservation but rather as a sign of its destruction,[47] and thus in these verses found a prophecy about the destruction of the Temple that had already been fulfilled. With their content focused on the past, verses 1 and 2 can be viewed as a form of introduction to consequential events that lead one to the city of Jerusalem where the drama of the Anti-Christ should take place in the future (Rev 11:3–4). Moreover Bousset presupposes the necessary assumption[48] that the writer of the Apocalypse himself did not originally attribute such events as these to the verses 1 and 2. This hypothesis is clearly marked with much difficulty. For example, one can object that with Rev 11:8 Jerusalem has been conceived of as still intact and standing, although the writer definitely speaks of what for him is an event of the future. Then again, one can hardly dispute this possibility. It is clear that the mention of the "outer courts of the Temple" with the past tense in the verse ἐδόθη τοῖς ἔθνεσιν (Rev 11:2) could well have placed the meaning and significance of these words in the past. But a definite analogy to the questionable meaning and understanding of 2 Thess 2:4 cannot at any event be derived from this passage.

Yet surely it is a different matter, as has just been alluded to, with the mention of Jerusalem in Rev 11:8 and with Rev 11:13,[49] if we may be permitted to add that verse. For here the city of which one tenth is to be destroyed and in which some seven thousand of its inhabitants are to perish by an earthquake can only in this context refer to the city of Jerusalem. The writer of the Christian Apocalypse has without doubt recorded prophecies after the year AD 70, whereby Jerusalem plays a role even though it was destroyed at that time. Concerning this nothing then is to be changed if Rev 11:8 ὅπου καὶ ὁ κύριος αὐτῶν ἐσταυρώθη might be an addition and the "large city" was originally intended to be Rome.[50] But all depends directly on the

---

46. Bousset, *Kommentar*, 374–75.

47. See Isa 34:10–11.

48. Bousset, *Kommentar*, 386.

49. Bleek, *Einleitung*, 723–24; Bousset, *Kommentar*, 505. A similar interpretation would apply to Rev 20:9. Cf. Bousset, 505. Bleek has found with Rev 20:9 evidence for the existence of the earthly Jerusalem during the time these words were written.

50. Spitta, *Die Offenbarung*, 112–13.

conception of the last writer. Owing to the circumstances he thought of Jerusalem, even if he may have adopted the entire prophecy with Christian imagery in an undoubtedly Christian form as we read from his text or even if he himself first placed the words, ὅπου καὶ ὁ κύριος αὐτῶν ἐσταυρώθη, in the text and perhaps set forth other changes to the original document.[51] But did he actually conceive of a rebuilt and restored Jerusalem or not? An elucidating remark or comment has not been made. But admittedly that does not mean or signify much, just as with 2 Thessalonians 2 any indication of the restoration of the Temple is completely lacking. This is to be concluded therefore because the writer of the Apocalypse followed the wording and structure of the older prophecies so closely, and not as rather it can be assumed with the writer of the Second Letter to the Thessalonians himself even if he actually used a written source.

So it would be conceivable that with the report and repetition of these prophecies he would have tacitly thought about the restoration of Jerusalem, particularly when he understood Rev 11:2 as an actual reference to the Temple. It would be difficult to say what source that expectation might have been taken from because this passage is not concerned here with a restored Jerusalem. Yet we appear to have an analogy here, just as we search for one. Nevertheless I do not venture to assert that. The writer might have been able to arrange these matters in his own manner and perhaps also with images and concepts that appear to us to be abstruse and convoluted. At all events from such a matter that is not so transparent, it is very difficult to attain any light for another realm of darkness.

Nevertheless with regard to the date for the Second Letter to the Thessalonians if it was actually written after AD 70, it appears to me that the most likely assumption would be that the writer wrote the words about the Temple simply because his document contained them (i.e., without at all thinking about the destruction of the Temple). From a general point of view this possibility is not to be disputed. It must be especially emphasized that the phrase, "The Temple of God," belonged to the characteristic vocabulary of the general Christian language of that time and expressed a reality of biblical history for every Christian. The more often and common it was to hear of the Temple and speak of it especially through the influence of the Old Testament, the more likely it became that the remembrance of the Temple was not related to the historical fact of its destruction, especially in a time in which this fact was no longer at all related to a recent

---

51. Bousset, *Kommentar*, 386.

event but lay already many decades in the past. Yet it should be added that this assumption is considerably more likely if the writer was dependent on a fixed, written document of the tradition rather than one that had been passed on orally. Such a fixed, written document generally tends to provide the propagator with greater authority. It is much easier to record the text without reflection and deliberation. But with an orally propagated tradition the question becomes especially difficult as to how the successive report of the destruction of the Temple could have remained intact as it wandered through many different, historical, intermediary stops on to the time of the writer. Thus we are led hereby to assume that there must have been an ongoing procurement of a written document. The possibility of this presumption has already been asserted above.

If then the letter was written after AD 70, one must render such an evaluation as presented above. But the question remains exactly that as to whether or not it could have been written after AD 70.

CONCLUSION

With regard to the preceding, laborious, and detailed presentation that I have believed this matter deserves, I hope that although the many considerations and proposals cannot have pleased the reader any more than myself, it nevertheless demonstrates better than complete certainty that I have not diminished the difficulty that verse 2 Thess 2:4 causes and affords the matter when a later date is given for the letter. It has been shown that our exegetical study has evolved and brought forth here a hypothesis that cannot be described and undertaken for the questionable verses and passages of our letter without the help of assumptions and thus without a certain degree of doubt, not to mention that they were actually suggested by the passage itself. Thus it must be conceded that one aspect remains that has not been convincingly explained and resolved with our exegetical study and that moreover will always easily allow for a certain amount of doubt.

All the same, however, I believe that the study offered above will not be overturned.

First of all, the prospect of evading the undeniable difficulty associated with 2 Thess 2:4 cannot lead us to change our conviction and judgment about the authenticity of the letter. With the assumption of actual authenticity, we are confronted with even more difficulties that are just as undeniable and that truly are of a completely different nature and meaning

The Authenticity of the Second Letter to the Thessalonians

such that they transform the letter into a mysterious riddle. I cannot present the evidence anew but I must ask the reader to allow the previously adduced arguments to have their full impact. The literary relationship of the Second Letter to the Thessalonians to the First Letter to the Thessalonians remains absolutely incomprehensible without the assumption of a forgery. For the most part it is essentially a matter of actual facts that occur as objective details and are independent of any subjective consideration and appraisal. Furthermore one is confronted not with just a few, single details, but rather with an abundance of conspicuous aspects in wording, in the composition of the text, in content, and in the structural posture of the letter. To admit and concede the authenticity would mean to give up and disregard the key reason for all of these similarities, for considering the Pauline corpus such a dependency of one of Paul's letters on another letter of his cannot be conceived. Moreover, it would also mean to disclaim and retract a satisfactory explanation of 2 Thess 2:2 as well as the closing remark of 2 Thess 3:17. Accordingly under these circumstances the doubt of the determination and viability of 2 Thess 2:4 is well-nigh called to bear; and since it may be possible that someone after the year AD 70 under certain stipulations could speak of the Temple of God, so the preponderance of reasons against the Pauline origin of the letter point further to the conclusion that this assumption should be accepted as a reality.

Admittedly a third point of view comes into question, according to which the letter would not have been written by Paul but nevertheless before the destruction of the Temple. Such a view would avoid all of the difficulties associated with both sides of the arguments already presented, and this may appear to be the best resolution. However, I believe that this way out is surely open to stronger reservations than our hypothesis for 2 Thess 2:4. The historical reasons that can be raised and brought to bear against such an early forgery[52] cannot be significantly attenuated over and against their factual significance. If the letter was actually intended for the community in Thessalonica, it is not understandable how it could have found acceptance there shortly after the death of Paul nor how the writer could have undertaken such a venture. If the destination for Thessalonica was only hypothetical, one does not at all understand how such a cover could have been selected at such an early date, for that presupposes a distribution and a considerable reputation for Paul's letters that can hardly be assumed before the year AD 70. We are thus hereby permitted to retain the view that

---

52. Cf. 36–39 above.

the falsified letter was written either toward the end of the first or at the beginning of the second century.

BIBLIOGRAPHY

Bahnsen. Untitled Entry. *JPT* VI (1880) 681ff.
Baumgarten and Crusius. Untitled Entry. See Bornemann.
Baur. *Paulus.* II 1845.
Beyschlag. Untitled Entry.
Blass. *Neutestamentliche Grammatik.*
Bleek and Mangold. *Einleitung in das Neue Testament.* 3rd ed.
Bonwetsch. *Studien zu den Kommentaren Hippolytus zum Buche Daniel und Hohen Liede.* *TUU* Neue Folge 1 73ff.
Bonwetsch and Achelis. Untitled Entry.
Bornemann. *Die Thessalonicherbriefe.* In MK 5th and 6th ed.
Bousset. *Der Antichrist.*
———. *Kommentar zur Offenbarung Johannnes.*
Brückner, W. *Die chronologische Reihenfolge in welcher die Briefe des Neuen Testaments verfasst sind.* Haarlem, 1890.
Burton. *Syntax of the Moods and Tenses in New Testament Greek.* 2nd ed. Edinburgh, 1894.
Buttmann, A. Untitled Entry.
Dick. *Der schriftstellerische Plural bei Paulus.* 1900.
Dobschütz. *Die urchristlichen Gemeinden.*
Düsterdieck. *Kommentar.*
Friedman and Grätz. "Die angebliche Fordauer des jüdischen Opferkultus nach der Zerstörung des zweiten Temples." *TJ* (1848) 338ff.
Grimm. "Die Echtheit der Briefe an die Thessalonicher." *SK* (1850) 789ff.
Grotius. Untitled Entry.
Gunkel. *Schöfung und Chaos.*
Harnack, Adolf. *Chronologie der altchristlichene Literatur.* I.
———. *Patristische Micellen.* TUU N. F. V 3, 86ff.
———. Untitled Entry. *TLZ* (1891) col 35f.
Helfe. Untitled Entry. *PAO* XXXVI (1847).
Hengstenberg, *Die Offenbarung des heiligen Johannes.* Berlin, 1849.
Hilgenfeld. *Einleitung in das Neue Testament.*
———. Untitled Entry. *ZWT* (1862).
Holtzmann, H. *Einleitung in das Neue Testament.*
———. *Lehrbuch der historisch-kritischen Einleitung in das Neue Testament.*
———. *Lehrbuch der Neutestamentlichen Theologie.*
———. Untitled Entry. In *HNT* 1.

———. Untitled Entry. In *SBL* V.
———. Untitled Entry. *TLZ* (1880) col 27.
———. "Zum zwieten Thessalonicherbrief." *ZNTW* II (1901) 97–108.
Jülicher. *Einleitung in das Neue Testament.*
———. *Die Gleichnisreden Jesu.*
Kern. "Über 2 Thess 2:1–12." *TZT* (1839) 145ff.
Klöpper. "Der zweite Brief an die Thessalonicher." *TSSO* II (1889).
Klostermann. *Das Markusevangelium.*
Laurent. Untitled Entry. *NTS.*
Malvenda, Thomas. *De Antichristo.* Lugdun. 1647.
Michelsen. Untitled Entry. See Schmiedel.
Otto. *De Epistola ad Diognetum.* Jena, 1844.
Pfleiderer. *Das Urchristentum.*
Rauch. Untitled Entry. *ZWT* (1895).
Reuss, E. *Die Geschichte der heiligen Schriften Neuen Testaments.*
Schmiedel. Untitled Entry. In *HNT* II 1 8–10.
Schott. *Epistolae Pauli ad Thessalonicenses et Galatas.* 1834.
Schürer. *Geschichte des jüdischen Volkes.* I.
Spitta. *Zur Geschichte und Literatur des Urchristentums.* 1893.
———. *Die Offenbarung des Jonannes.*
Theodoret and Theophylact. Untitled Entry.
Tillemont. Untitled Entry.
Uhlhorn. Untitled Entry. *NZHT* (1851) 322.
Victorin. *Apokalypsenkommentar.*
von Hofmann. *Die heilige Schriften Neuen Testaments.* I.
Wabnitz. Untitled Entry. *JPT* (1884) 512ff; (1885) 134ff.
Weiss, B. *Einleitung in das Neue Testament.*
Weizsäcker. *Das Apostolische Zeitalter.*
Wernle, *Die Anfänge unserer Religion.*
Westrik. *De echtheid van den tweeden brief aan de Thessalonicensen.* Utrecht, 1879.
Zahn. "Apokalyptische Studien" ("Nero der Antichrist"). ZKWKL (1886) 337ff.
———. *Einleitung in das Neue Testament.* 1st ed.
———. *Die Geschichte des Kanons.*
———. *Ignatius von Antiochien.* 1873.
———. *Patr Apost Opp.*

You might also be interested in:

The Messianic Secret
Das Messiasgeheimnis in den Evangelien
by William Wrede

PB ISBN: 978 0 22717683 2
PDF ISBN: 978 0 227 90671 2
Kindle ISBN: 978 0 227 90673 6
ePub ISBN: 978 0 227 90672 9

A ground-breaking academic study of whether Jesus actively identified himself as the Messiah. Available in English with the translation by J.C.G. Greig, *The Messianic Secret* is still the point of departure for all studies of the Gospel of Mark and of an understanding of the literary methods of the Gospel writers.

Wrede's primary concern in his discussion of Mark is the doctrine of the messianic secret, the notion of a Jesus who, assuming messiahship at baptism, keeps it secret until, after the confessions of Peter, he introduces the disciples to the idea of a suffering and dying Messiah. The idea of such a secret can be shown, from a study of the other Gospels, to have developed variously, and above all to go back to a period prior to Mark's work as the earliest evangelist.

Wrede finds the theological source of the idea of a secret in a contrast between what the Church came to think of Jesus and how his life had been understood during his ministry. He suggests that because the Church came to think of Jesus as Messiah after the Resurrection, they came to explain the lack of explicit declaration of his messiahship by Jesus during his ministry by suggesting that (nevertheless) Jesus had after all secretly revealed himself as the Messiah.

Wrede was among the first to recognise the creative contribution of the writers of the Gospels, and to emphasise the necessity of a historical approach to the Church's traditions if we are to avoid a naive misunderstanding of the perspective from which the Gospels are written. His work is thus the foundation stone not only in the study of Mark, but also in the vexed area of the contribution of the evangelists to the Gospel. In this field Wrede's work is still essential reading, unsurpassed by the more advanced literary critics of the present day.

*First published in 1987,
reprinted in 2018.*